National 5
Geography
Practice Papers for SQA Exams

Sheena Williamson

Contents

HODDER GIBSON
AN HACHETTE UK COMPANY

The Publishers would like to thank the following for permission to reproduce copyright material:

Exam rubrics at the start of Section 1, Section 2 and Section 3 of each practice paper are reproduced by kind permission of SQA, Copyright © Scottish Qualifications Authority.

Ordnance Survey maps on pages 2–3, 10–11, 22–23, 24–25, 44–45, 52–53 are reproduced by permission of Ordnance Survey on behalf of HMSO. © Crown copyright 2016. All rights reserved. Ordnance Survey Licence number 100047450.

Photo credits: p.8 (tl) © Anirut Rassameesritrakool/123RF, (tr) © Oleksandr Ivanchenko/Alamy Stock Photo, (bl) ©shootsphot/123RF, (br) © John Morrison/Alamy Stock Photo; p.34 © Shutterstock/Evgeny Sribnyjj; p.38 © Jeff Schmaltz, LANCE/EOSDIS Rapid Response/NASA; p.40 © jcg_oida – Fotolia; p.55 © Pawel Bienkowski/Alamy Stock Photo; p.57 © Carl Court/Getty Images.

Every effort has been made to trace all copyright holders, but if any have been inadvertently overlooked the Publishers will be pleased to make the necessary arrangements at the first opportunity.

Although every effort has been made to ensure that website addresses are correct at time of going to press, Hodder Gibson cannot be held responsible for the content of any website mentioned in this book. It is sometimes possible to find a relocated web page by typing in the address of the home page for a website in the URL window of your browser.

Hachette UK's policy is to use papers that are natural, renewable and recyclable products and made from wood grown in sustainable forests. The logging and manufacturing processes are expected to conform to the environmental regulations of the country of origin.

Orders: please contact Bookpoint Ltd, 130 Park Drive, Milton Park, Abingdon, Oxon OX14 4SE. Telephone: (44) 01235 827720. Fax: (44) 01235 400454. Lines are open 9.00–5.00, Monday to Saturday, with a 24-hour message answering service. Visit our website at www.hoddereducation.co.uk. Hodder Gibson can be contacted direct on: Tel: 0141 333 4650; Fax: 0141 404 8188; email: hoddergibson@hodder.co.uk

© Sheena Williamson 2016
First published in 2016 by
Hodder Gibson, an imprint of Hodder Education,
An Hachette UK Company
211 St Vincent Street
Glasgow G2 5QY

Impression number   5 4 3 2 1
Year   2020 2019 2018 2017 2016

Cover photo © Lightwise/123RF.com
Illustrations by Aptara, Inc.
Typeset in Din regular 12/14.4 pts. by Aptara, Inc.
Printed and bound by CPI Group (UK) Ltd, Croydon, CR0 4YY

A catalogue record for this title is available from the British Library

ISBN: 978 1 4718 8592 1

Introduction

National 5 Geography

Course assessment

The Course assessment will consist of two parts: a question paper (60 marks) and an assignment (20 marks). The two marks are added together to give a total out of 80. The question paper is therefore worth 75% of the overall marks for the Course assessment and the assignment worth 25%.

The question paper

The purpose of the question paper is to allow you to demonstrate the skills you have acquired and to show your knowledge and understanding from across the topics you have covered in the course. The question paper will give you the chance to show your ability in handling maps, diagrams and graphs as well as describing, explaining and analysing information from the topics you have studied.

The question paper has three sections. In section 1, you will have a choice of question depending on the landscape type you have studied and then you must answer all other questions. In section 2 you must answer all questions. In section 3 there are six questions and you must answer two from the six options.

Section 1: Physical Environments is worth 20 marks. In this section you can be asked questions on the topics of Weather, Landscape types, Land uses and Conflicts. You will have studied two landscape types, either Glaciated Landscapes and Coastal Landscapes (normally question 1) or Upland Limestone Landscapes and River and Valley Landscapes (normally question 2). You may be asked to explain formations of features, for example corries, as well as explaining the processes involved in their formation. You may be asked to show your skills acquired throughout the course by assessing the suitability of a map area for a particular land use, for example recreation and tourism. In this section there is likely to be a physical question based on an Ordnance Survey map.

Section 2: Human Environments is worth 20 marks. In this section you can be asked questions on the topics of Population, Urban Studies and Rural Studies. Questions can relate to both developed and developing countries. You may be asked to show your skills acquired throughout the course by assessing the land uses found in a particular area on a map. In this section there is likely to be a human question based on an Ordnance Survey map.

Section 3: Global Issues is worth 20 marks. In this section you have a choice. You should answer two questions from a choice of six. The Global Issues choices are: Climate Change; Impact of Human Activity on the Natural Environment; Environmental Hazards; Trade and Globalisation; Tourism; and Health. Each question has the same level of difficulty – there is no question easier or more difficult than another. There are usually two parts to each question. Part A usually has a graph, diagram or a map for you to describe, using the information on it, and is worth 4 marks. Part B is an explanation or assessment of the particular topic and is worth 6 marks. In total each question is worth 10 marks.

For more detailed information on the topics you will be assessed on in the exam go to the SQA website and search for the Geography area (www.sqa.org.uk).

The assignment

The assignment is completed throughout the year and submitted to SQA to be marked around March time. This is worth 20 marks. Marks are awarded for the demonstration of skills as well as knowledge and understanding of your chosen topic.

Common errors

Choices

The paper has a choice of questions. In the Physical section make sure you do **either** Q1 **or** Q2, not both.

In the Global Issues section you only need to complete **two** questions. You will use up valuable time if you answer all the questions and you may not have the time to put in the detail needed to gain full marks for the two questions required.

Detail

The way to achieve full marks is to put as much detail as you can into your answer. Detail equals marks which will improve your overall grade. Marks are frequently lost because questions often ask you to refer to an example you have studied and you will lose at least 1 mark if you give a general answer. At the beginning of your answer you should state the case study you are going to talk about and by giving specific detail the examiner will be aware of your breadth of knowledge. A good guide to how much to write is to look at the number of marks allocated to each question. If the question is worth 6 marks then you should try to make at least six points in your answer.

Bullet points/lists

If you use bullet points or a list you may lose marks. In a 6 mark question you may only gain 1 mark out of 6 for a list. For example, heart disease is caused by smoking, drinking, bad diet and being overweight (1 mark). However, what you should do is expand your answer so you get 1 mark for each cause, i.e.:

Too much saturated fat can cause hardening of the arteries or block the arteries leading to heart disease **(1)**. The carbon monoxide in tobacco smoke reduces the amount of oxygen in your blood. This means your heart has to pump harder to supply the body with the oxygen it needs **(1)**. Stress can cause abnormal heart rhythms, high blood pressure and damage to your heart muscle **(1)**. Being overweight or obese can lead to a build-up of plaque in your arteries. Eventually, an area of plaque can rupture, causing a blood clot to form **(1)**.

By putting detail into the list you can increase your mark from 1 to 6!

Read the question

Read the question carefully. If you go off at a tangent you may get no marks. Be especially careful in topics such as Population and Farming – they can ask for either developed or developing countries.

If you are asked to explain, make sure you give reasons and not just description, otherwise you could lose most of the marks. This is particularly relevant in Weather questions. If you are asked to explain the weather conditions you must give reasons for the weather being experienced, not just describe the actual weather.

In Part A of the Global Issues questions you will be asked to describe a graph, map, diagram etc. You will get no marks for explanation so there is no need to waste time which can be used to complete other questions.

Avoid repetition

Try not to repeat yourself. You will gain no extra marks for repeating the same information in a different way. You could use this time to complete another answer or check over your other answers.

Writing

Try to be as neat as possible and make your writing legible. Always use a blue or a black pen in the exam. The answer papers are scanned so using blue or black makes your answers clearer.

The exam

Duration: 1 hour, 45 minutes

Total marks: 60

Section 1	Physical Environments	20 marks
Section 2	Human Environments	20 marks
Section 3	Global Issues	20 marks

Section 1

Attempt **either** Q1 **or** Q2 then Q3, Q4 and Q5.

Section 2

Attempt all questions (Q6, Q7, Q8).

Section 3

Attempt any two questions from:

- Q9 – Climate Change
- Q10 – Impact of Human Activity on the Natural Environment
- Q11 – Environmental Hazards
- Q12 – Trade and Globalisation
- Q13 – Tourism
- Q14 – Health

Remember, you can use sketches, maps and diagrams (labelled appropriately) in your answer, where relevant. Remember to identify which question you are answering in your answer booklet.

Make sure in the Global Issues section that you identify the questions you are going to answer by the topic, for example, by Climate Change and not by the question number (such as Q9) as this could change.

Revision grid

	Paper A	Paper B	Paper C
PHYSICAL ENVIRONMENTS			
Ordnance Survey	Yes	Yes	Yes
Landscape Types			
Identifying features	OS - Q1a , Q2, Q3a	OS - Q1a, Q2a	OS - Q1a, Q2a
Formation of glacial features	Q1b	Q1b	
Formation of river features	Q2b		Q2b
Formation of coastal features			Q1b
Formation of limestone features		Q2b	
Landscape land use	Q3	Q3	Q3, Q5
Land use conflicts	Q4		Q5
Weather			
Factors affecting local weather conditions		Q4	
Synoptic chart–depressions and anticyclones	Q5		
Depressions		Q5	
Anticyclones			Q4
HUMAN ENVIRONMENTS			
Ordnance Survey	Yes	Yes	Yes
Population			
Indicators of development	Q7a, Q7b		
Changes in birth and death rates			Q8
Population pyramids		Q7a	
Effects of population change		Q7b	
Urban			
Characteristics of land use zones	Q6 OS		Q6a OS
Recent developments in land use zones	Q8	Q6 OS	Q6b OS
Shanty town improvements			Q7
Rural			
Modern developments in farming in developing countries		Q8	
GLOBAL ISSUES			
Handling Information			
Pie chart	Q9a	Q9a,Q12a	Q9a, Q12a
Map	Q11a, Q14a	Q10a, Q11a, Q14a	Q11a, Q14a
Line graph	Q12a		

	Paper A	Paper B	Paper C
Bar graph	Q10a, Q13a		Q10a
Divided bar graph			Q13a
Table		Q13a	
Climate Change			
Managing climate change	Q9b		
Causes of climate change		Q9b	
Local and global effects of climate change			Q9b
Impact of Human Activity on the Natural Environment			
Effects of human activity on the rainforest or tundra	Q10b		
Advantages/disadvantages of deforestation in the rainforest		Q10b	
Causes of land degradation in the rainforest			Q10b
Environmental Hazards			
Strategies to reduce effects of hazard	Q11b		
Impact of a tropical storm		Q11b	
Predicting and planning for an environmental hazard			Q11b
Trade and Globalisation			
Inequalities in trade	Q12b		
Fair trade		Q12b	
Effects of changing demand for a product in a developing country			Q12b
Tourism			
Impact of mass tourism	Q13b		
Growth of mass tourism		Q13b	
Ecotourism			Q13b
Health			
Methods to control disease – AIDS	Q14b		
Effects of malaria cholera/ kwashiorkor/pneumonia		Q14b	
Causes of heart disease, cancer or asthma			Q14b

National 5 Geography

HODDER
GIBSON
LEARN MORE

OS map showing Dingwall
Extract reproduced by permission of Ordnance Survey on behalf of HMSO. © Crown copyright 2016.
All rights reserved. Ordnance Survey Licence number 100047450.

ROADS AND PATHS

Not necessarily rights of way

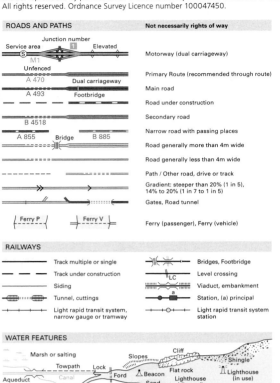

Junction number	
Service area / Elevated	
M1	
Unfenced	
A 470	Motorway (dual carriageway)
	Dual carriageway
A 493	Primary Route (recommended through route)
	Footbridge
	Main road
B 4518	Road under construction
	Secondary road
A 855	Bridge	B 885
	Narrow road with passing places
	Road generally more than 4m wide
	Road generally less than 4m wide
	Path / Other road, drive or track
	Gradient: steeper than 20% (1 in 5),
	14% to 20% (1 in 7 to 1 in 5)
	Gates, Road tunnel
Ferry P	Ferry V
	Ferry (passenger), Ferry (vehicle)

RAILWAYS

	Track multiple or single		Bridges, Footbridge
	Track under construction	LC	Level crossing
	Siding	a	Viaduct, embankment
	Tunnel, cuttings	a	Station, (a) principal
	Light rapid transit system, narrow gauge or tramway		Light rapid transit system station

WATER FEATURES

Marsh or salting, Slopes, Cliff, Shingle, Towpath, Lock, Aqueduct, Canal, Ford, Beacon, Flat rock, Lighthouse, Weir, Sand, Lighthouse (disused), Lighthouse (in use), Lake, Footbridge, Bridge, Normal tidal limit, Dunes, Mud, Low water mark, High water mark, Canal (dry)

HEIGHTS

1 metre = 3·2808 feet	
50	Contours are at 10 metres vertical interval
·144	Heights are to the nearest metre above mean sea level

Where two heights are shown the first height is to the base of the triangulation pillar and the second (in brackets) to the highest natural point of the hill

ROCK FEATURES

Outcrop, Cliff, Scree

PUBLIC RIGHTS OF WAY

············	Footpath
– – – – –	Bridleway
– · – · – · –	Restricted byway
–+–+–+–+–	Byway open to all traffic

The symbols show the defined route so far as the scale of mapping will allow.

The representation on this map of any other road, track or path is no evidence of the existence of a right of way. Not shown on maps of Scotland

Danger Area — Firing and Test Ranges in the area. Danger! Observe warning notices.

BOUNDARIES

–+–+–+	National
–+–+–+	District
–··–··–··	County, Unitary Authority, Metropolitan District or London Borough
	National Park

OTHER PUBLIC ACCESS

· · · ·	Other route with public access (not normally shown in urban areas). Alignments are based on the best information available. These routes are not shown on maps of Scotland.
● ● ●	On-road cycle route
○ ○ ○	Traffic-free cycle route
[4]	National Cycle Network number
[8]	Regional Cycle Network number
◆ ◆	National Trail, European Long Distance Path, Long Distance Route, selected Recreational Routes

ANTIQUITIES

+	Site of antiquity
⚔	Battlefield (with date)
☆ ····	Visible earthwork
VILLA	Roman
Castle	Non-Roman

TOURIST INFORMATION

⚑ 🚐 🚐	Camp site / caravan site
✿	Garden
Γ	Golf course or links
🅸 🅸	Information centre (all year / seasonal)
⚘	Nature reserve
P P&R	Parking, Park and ride (all year / seasonal)
✕	Picnic site
Ⓚ	Recreation / leisure / sports centre
▨	Selected places of tourist interest
☎ ☎	Telephone, public / roadside assistance
☼	Viewpoint
Ⓥ	Visitor centre
!	Walks / Trails
◎	World Heritage site or area
▲	Youth hostel

LAND FEATURES

⟝–––⟞	Electricity transmission line (pylons shown at standard spacing)
> --> -->	Pipe line (arrow indicates direction of flow)
ruin	Buildings
	Important building (selected)
⬤	Bus or coach station
⬧	Current or former place of worship / with tower
⬧	with spire, minaret or dome
+	Place of worship
⬦	Glass structure
Ⓗ	Heliport
△	Triangulation pillar
⊤	Mast
ⵡ ⵡ	Wind pump, wind turbine
ⵚ	Windmill with or without sails
+	Graticule intersection at 5' intervals
⸬⸬⸬	Cutting, embankment
⁙⁙	Landfill site or slag/spoil heap
	Coniferous wood
	Non-coniferous wood
	Mixed wood
	Orchard
	Park or ornamental ground
🄰	Forestry Commission land
	National Trust (always open / limited access, observe local signs)
	National Trust for Scotland (always open / limited access, observe local signs)

ABBREVIATIONS

Br	Bridge	MS	Milestone
Cemy	Cemetery	Mus	Museum
CG	Cattle grid	P	Post office
CH	Clubhouse	PC	Public convenience (in rural areas)
Fm	Farm	PH	Public house
Ho	House	Sch	School
MP	Milepost	TH	Town Hall, Guildhall or equivalent

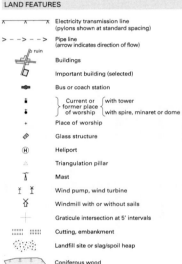

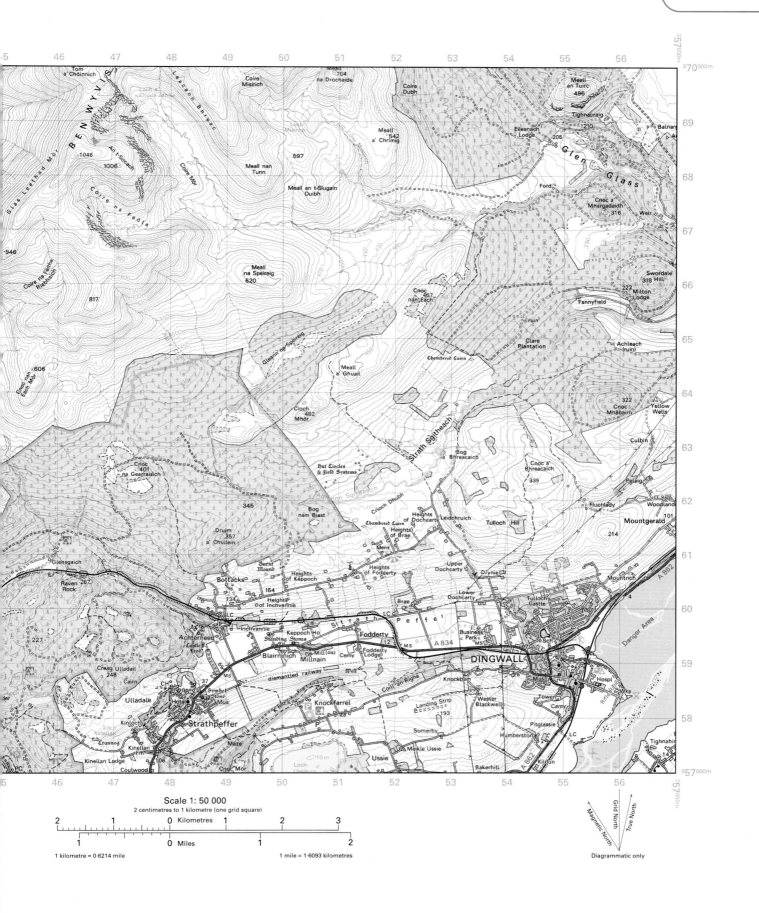

Scale 1: 50 000

2 centimetres to 1 kilometre (one grid square)

2   1   0   Kilometres   1   2   3

1   0   Miles   1   2

1 kilometre = 0·6214 mile   1 mile = 1·6093 kilometres

Magnetic North
Grid North
True North

Diagrammatic only

Duration: 1 hour, 45 minutes

Total marks: 60

SECTION 1 – PHYSICAL ENVIRONMENTS – 20 MARKS

Attempt EITHER question 1 OR question 2. ALSO attempt questions 3, 4 and 5.

SECTION 2 – HUMAN ENVIRONMENTS – 20 MARKS

Attempt questions 6, 7 and 8.

SECTION 3 – GLOBAL ISSUES – 20 MARKS

Attempt any TWO of the following:

Question 9 – Climate Change

Question 10 – Impact of Human Activity on the Natural Environment

Question 11 – Environmental Hazards

Question 12 – Trade and Globalisation

Question 13 – Tourism

Question 14 – Health

Remember, you can use sketches, maps and diagrams (labelled appropriately) in your answer, where relevant. Remember to identify which question you are answering in your answer booklet.

Section 1: Physical Environments

Total marks: 20

Attempt EITHER question 1 OR question 2 AND questions 3, 4 and 5.

		MARKS	STUDENT MARGIN
Question 1	**Glaciated Uplands**		

Study the Ordnance Survey map extract of the Dingwall area.

a) Match the glaciated upland features shown below with the correct grid reference.

Features: truncated spur, corrie, U-shaped valley

Choose from grid references:

467677

476683

525594

435663 — **3**

HTP Chapter 1.2 Page 9

b) **Explain** the formation of a corrie.

You may use a diagram(s) in your answer. — **4**

[Now answer questions 3, 4 and 5]

MARKS   STUDENT MARGIN

[Do not answer this question if you have already answered Question 1]

Question 2   **Rivers and Valleys**

Study the Ordnance Survey map extract of the Dingwall area.

a)   Match the river features shown below with the correct grid reference.

Features: V-shaped valley, meander, tributary

Choose from grid references:

528595

442591

447585

473657   3

b)   **Explain** the formation of a waterfall.

You may use a diagram(s) in your answer.   4

[Now answer questions 3, 4 and 5]

HTP
Chapter 1.2
Page 16

Question 3   **Diagram Q3: Land uses in the map extract area**

Landscape uses **?**

Industry
Water storage and supply
Farming   Forestry
Renewable energy
Recreation and tourism **?**

Look at Diagram Q3.

Choose one land use from Diagram Q3. Using map evidence **explain** the advantages the area of the map extract has for your chosen land use.

5

Question 4   Diagram Q4: Selected land use conflicts

Landscape Types
Glaciated uplands
Upland limestone
Coastal landscapes
Rivers and valleys

HTP
Chapter 1.4
Page 24/25

Study Diagram Q4.

Choose one landscape type from Diagram Q4 and, referring to
an area you have studied, **explain** strategies which can be
used to reduce land use conflicts in your chosen area.

4

Question 5   Diagram Q5A: Synoptic chart, 25 July 2016

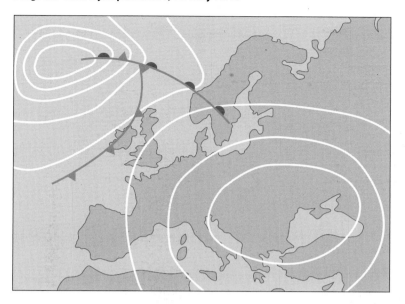

Diagram Q5B: Weather forecast for the Mediterranean and the UK

High pressure looks set to continue in the Mediterranean for the rest of the month. It should be dry with mainly clear skies and long spells of sunshine. Temperatures are expected to be around 27°C, the average for this time of the year. In the UK, changeable conditions will persist. Temperatures should average around 14°C. Northern and western parts of the UK could see spells of rain and wind at times.

MARKS

STUDENT MARGIN

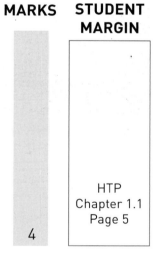

HTP
Chapter 1.1
Page 5

Study Diagrams Q5A and Q5B.

Explain the forecasts for the Mediterranean area and the UK. You should refer to the synoptic chart in your answer.

4

[Now go to Section 2]

OS map showing Preston

Extract reproduced by permission of Ordnance Survey on behalf of HMSO. © Crown copyright 2016.
All rights reserved. Ordnance Survey Licence number 100047450.

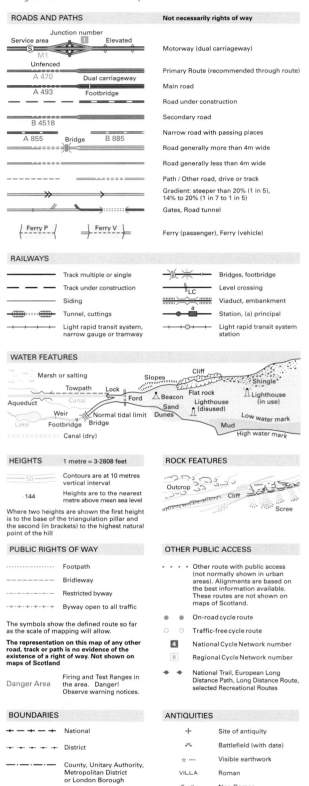

ROADS AND PATHS
Not necessarily rights of way

Motorway (dual carriageway)	
Primary Route (recommended through route)	
Main road	
Road under construction	
Secondary road	
Narrow road with passing places	
Road generally more than 4m wide	
Road generally less than 4m wide	
Path / Other road, drive or track	
Gradient: steeper than 20% (1 in 5), 14% to 20% (1 in 7 to 1 in 5)	
Gates, Road tunnel	
Ferry (passenger), Ferry (vehicle)	

Service area (S) · Junction number · Elevated · M1 · Unfenced · A 470 · Dual carriageway · A 493 · Footbridge · B 4518 · A 855 · Bridge · B 885 · Ferry P · Ferry V

RAILWAYS

Track multiple or single		Bridges, footbridge	
Track under construction		Level crossing (LC)	
Siding		Viaduct, embankment	
Tunnel, cuttings		Station, (a) principal	
Light rapid transit system, narrow gauge or tramway		Light rapid transit system station	

WATER FEATURES

Marsh or salting · Cliff · Slopes · Shingle · Towpath · Lock · Flat rock · Lighthouse (in use) · Aqueduct · Canal · Ford · Beacon · Lighthouse (disused) · Sand · Weir · Dunes · Low water mark · Lake · Footbridge · Bridge · Normal tidal limit · Mud · High water mark · Canal (dry)

HEIGHTS
1 metre = 3·2808 feet

50 — Contours are at 10 metres vertical interval

·144 — Heights are to the nearest metre above mean sea level

Where two heights are shown the first height is to the base of the triangulation pillar and the second (in brackets) to the highest natural point of the hill

ROCK FEATURES

Outcrop · Cliff · Scree

PUBLIC RIGHTS OF WAY

· · · · · ·	Footpath
– – – –	Bridleway
— — —	Restricted byway
–·+·+·+·+·+·	Byway open to all traffic

The symbols show the defined route so far as the scale of mapping will allow.

The representation on this map of any other road, track or path is no evidence of the existence of a right of way. Not shown on maps of Scotland

Danger Area — Firing and Test Ranges in the area. Danger! Observe warning notices.

OTHER PUBLIC ACCESS

· · · · Other route with public access (not normally shown in urban areas). Alignments are based on the best information available. These routes are not shown on maps of Scotland.

●—● On-road cycle route

○—○ Traffic-free cycle route

[4] National Cycle Network number

[8] Regional Cycle Network number

◆—◆ National Trail, European Long Distance Path, Long Distance Route, selected Recreational Routes

BOUNDARIES

—+——+—+—	National
—·+·+·+·—	District
—·——·——·—	County, Unitary Authority, Metropolitan District or London Borough
	National Park

ANTIQUITIES

+	Site of antiquity
⚔	Battlefield (with date)
☼ ····	Visible earthwork
VILLA	Roman
Castle	Non-Roman

TOURIST INFORMATION

Camp site / caravan site	
Garden	
Golf course or links	
Information centre (all year / seasonal)	
Nature reserve	
Parking, Park and ride (all year / seasonal)	
Picnic site	
Recreation / leisure / sports centre	
Selected places of tourist interest	
Telephone, public / roadside assistance	
Viewpoint	
Visitor centre	
Walks / Trails	
World Heritage site or area	
Youth hostel	

LAND FEATURES

Electricity transmission line (pylons shown at standard spacing)	
Pipe line (arrow indicates direction of flow)	
Buildings	
Important building (selected)	
Bus or coach station	
Current or former place of worship: with tower / with spire, minaret or dome	
Place of worship	
Glass structure	
Heliport	
Triangulation pillar	
Mast	
Wind pump, wind turbine	
Windmill with or without sails	
Graticule intersection at 5' intervals	
Cutting, embankment	
Landfill site or slag/spoil heap	
Coniferous wood	
Non-coniferous wood	
Mixed wood	
Orchard	
Park or ornamental ground	
Forestry Commission land	
National Trust (always open / limited access, observe local signs)	
National Trust for Scotland (always open / limited access, observe local signs)	

ABBREVIATIONS

Br	Bridge	MS	Milestone
Cemy	Cemetery	Mus	Museum
CG	Cattle grid	P	Post office
CH	Clubhouse	PC	Public convenience (in rural areas)
Fm	Farm	PH	Public house
Ho	House	Sch	School
MP	Milepost	TH	Town Hall, Guildhall or equivalent

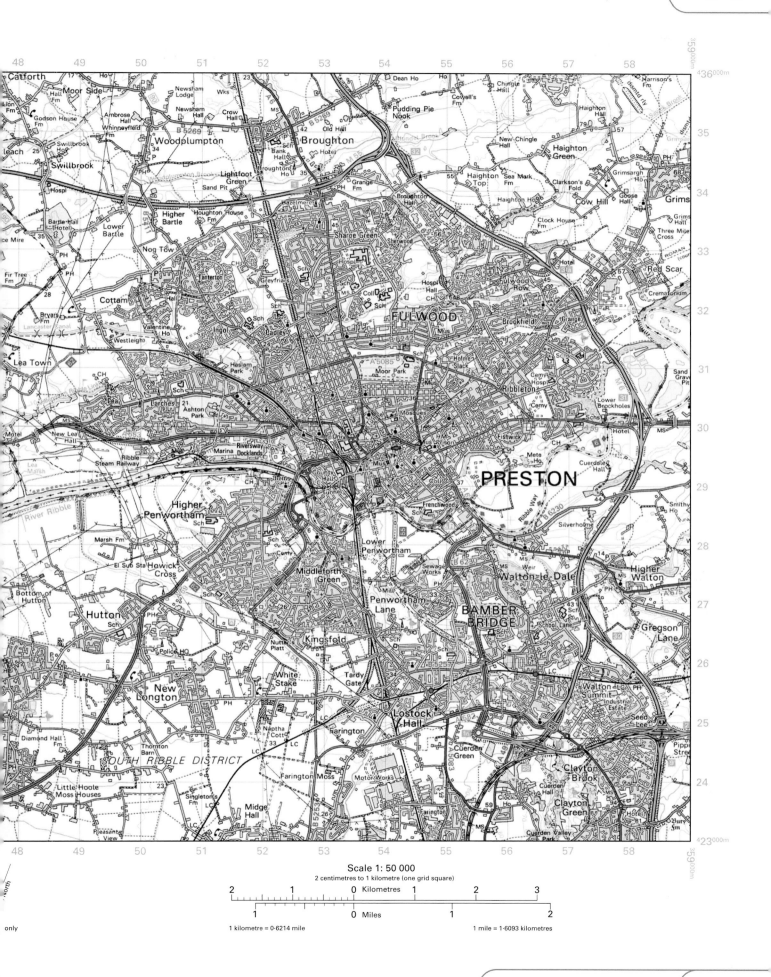

Scale 1: 50 000
2 centimetres to 1 kilometre (one grid square)

2   1   0 Kilometres   1   2   3

1   0 Miles   1   2

1 kilometre = 0·6214 mile   1 mile = 1·6093 kilometres

Section 2: Human Environments

Total marks: 20

Attempt questions 6, 7 and 8.

MARKS STUDENT MARGIN

Question 6 Diagram Q6: Selected land use zones in Preston

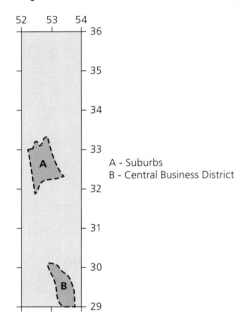

A - Suburbs
B - Central Business District

Study Diagram Q6 and the Ordnance Survey map extract of the Preston area.

Mr Bailey's S4 class has completed an urban land use survey for their National 5 assignment. They visited the CBD and the suburbs of Preston. Using map evidence, describe, in detail, the main features they found in both land use zones.

5

HTP
Chapter 2.2
Page 44/46

MARKS   **STUDENT MARGIN**

Question 7   Diagram Q7: Selected indicators of development for the UK and Chad

Indicators	UK	Chad
GNP per capita	$37,000	$826
Literacy rate	99%	47%
People per doctor	400	20,000
Life expectancy	81	51
% employed in agriculture	1%	78%

Study Diagram Q7.

a) **Describe**, **in detail**, the differences in development between Chad and the United Kingdom.

3

HTP
Chapter 2.1
Page 33/35

b) Choose **two** indicators from Diagram Q7. For each indicator give reasons for the differences between a developed country like the UK and a developing country like Chad.

6

Question 8   Diagram Q8: Land use on the rural/urban fringe

MARKS

STUDENT MARGIN

Look at Diagram Q8.

Land use in the countryside is changing. Give reasons why airports, business parks, golf courses and housing are attracted to the rural/urban fringe.

6

HTP
Chapter 2.2
Page 50/51

[Now go to Section 3]

Section 3: Global Issues

Total marks: 20

Attempt any TWO questions.

Question 9 – Climate Change

Question 10 – Impact of Human Activity on the Natural Environment

Question 11 – Environmental Hazards

Question 12 - Trade and Globalisation

Question 13 – Tourism

Question 14 – Health

Question 9   Climate Change

Diagram Q9A: Greenhouse gas emissions

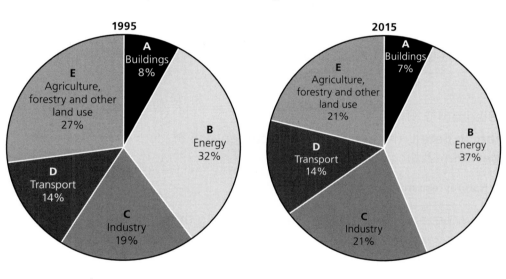

a)   Study Diagram Q9A.

Describe, in detail, the changes in greenhouse gas emissions between 1995 and 2015.

4

HTP
Chapter 3.1
Page 62

Diagram Q9B: Some effects of climate change

Sea level rise: according to UK Met Office, sea levels around the UK have risen about 10 centimetres since 1900.

Changes in rainfall: rainfall in the UK during summer is decreasing, while in winter it is increasing.

UK Met Office

b)   Look at Diagram Q9B.

Describe, **in detail**, ways in which people try to manage climate change.

6

MARKS | STUDENT MARGIN

Question 10 Impact of Human Activity on the Natural Environment

Diagram Q10A: Percentage ice cover 2000–2015

HTP Chapter 3.2 Page 68/69

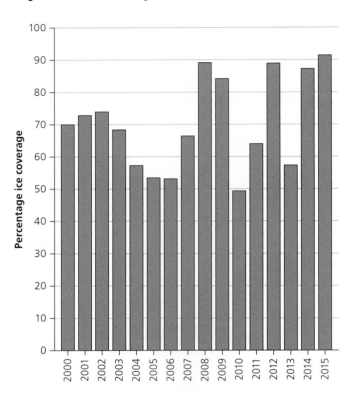

a) Study Diagram Q10A.

Describe, in detail, the changes in the percentage of ice cover between 2000 and 2015. 4

Diagram Q10B: Natural resources

Natural resources: any natural substance that living things can use Examples: air, water, sunlight, soil, minerals, plants, animals, forests, fossil fuels

b) Look at Diagram Q10B.

For **either** the rainforest **or** the tundra, **explain** ways in which recent human activities affect the people and the environment of your chosen area. 6

Question 11 Environmental Hazards

Diagram Q11: Active volcanoes

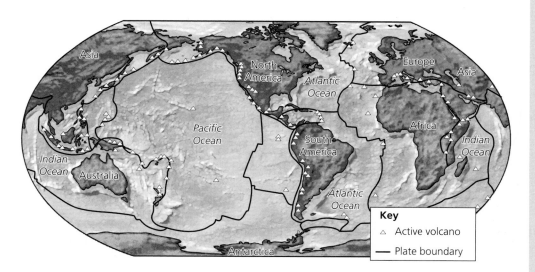

Study Diagram Q11.

a) **Describe**, **in detail**, the distribution of the Earth's active volcanoes.

4

b) Referring to a named hurricane, earthquake or volcano you have studied, **explain** strategies used to reduce its effects.

6

HTP
Chapter 3.3
Page 79/80

Question 12 Trade and Globalisation

Diagram Q12A: Changing percentage volume of world trade

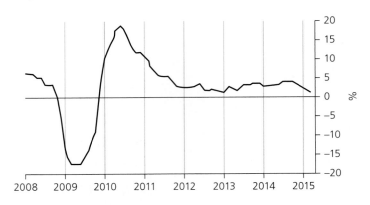

a) Study Diagram Q12A.

Describe, in detail, the changes in the percentage volume of world trade between 2008 and 2015.

Diagram Q12B: Share of world trade/GDP

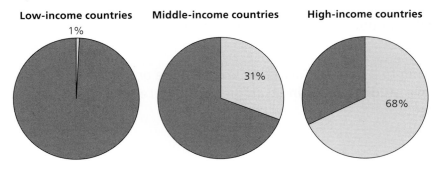

b) Look at Diagram Q12B.

Explain the causes of inequalities in world trade.

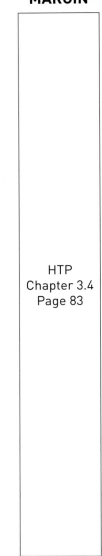

MARKS	STUDENT MARGIN
4	HTP Chapter 3.4 Page 83
6	

Question 13 Tourism

Diagram Q13: Selected international tourist arrivals 1990–2014

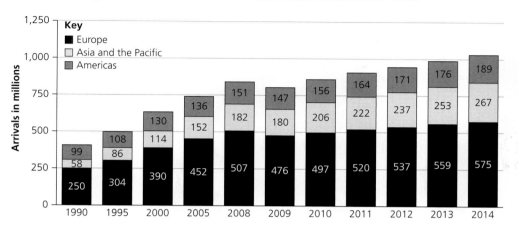

Study Diagram Q13.

a) **Describe, in detail**, the changes in international tourist arrivals 1990–2014.

4

b) **Explain** the impact of mass tourism on the people and environment.

You should refer to areas you have studied in your answer.

6

Question 14 Health

Diagram Q14A: Access to health care

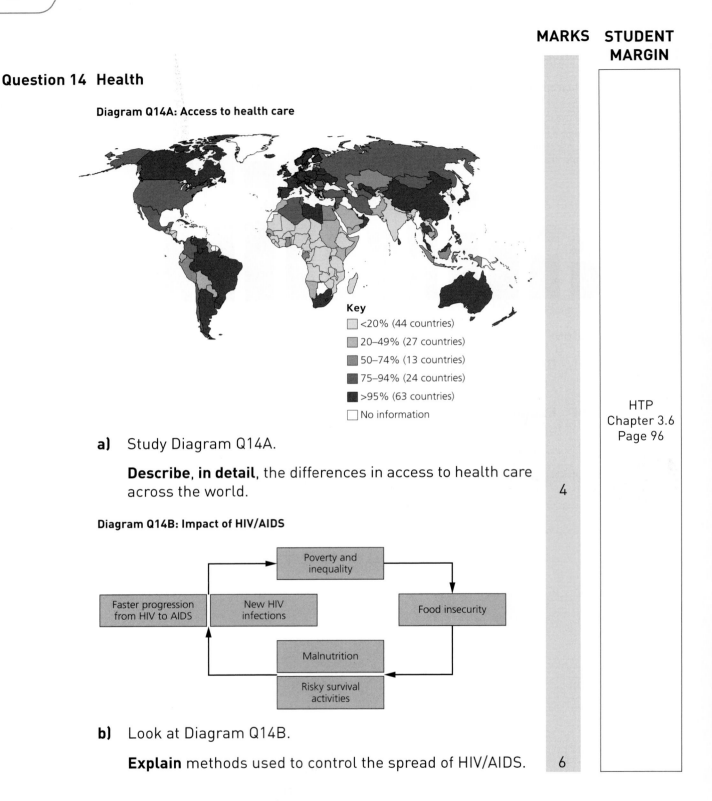

Key
☐ <20% (44 countries)
☐ 20–49% (27 countries)
☐ 50–74% (13 countries)
☐ 75–94% (24 countries)
☐ >95% (63 countries)
☐ No information

a) Study Diagram Q14A.

Describe, **in detail**, the differences in access to health care across the world.

4

Diagram Q14B: Impact of HIV/AIDS

Poverty and inequality

Faster progression from HIV to AIDS

New HIV infections

Food insecurity

Malnutrition

Risky survival activities

b) Look at Diagram Q14B.

Explain methods used to control the spread of HIV/AIDS.

6

HTP
Chapter 3.6
Page 96

[End of Practice Paper A]

National 5
Geography

B

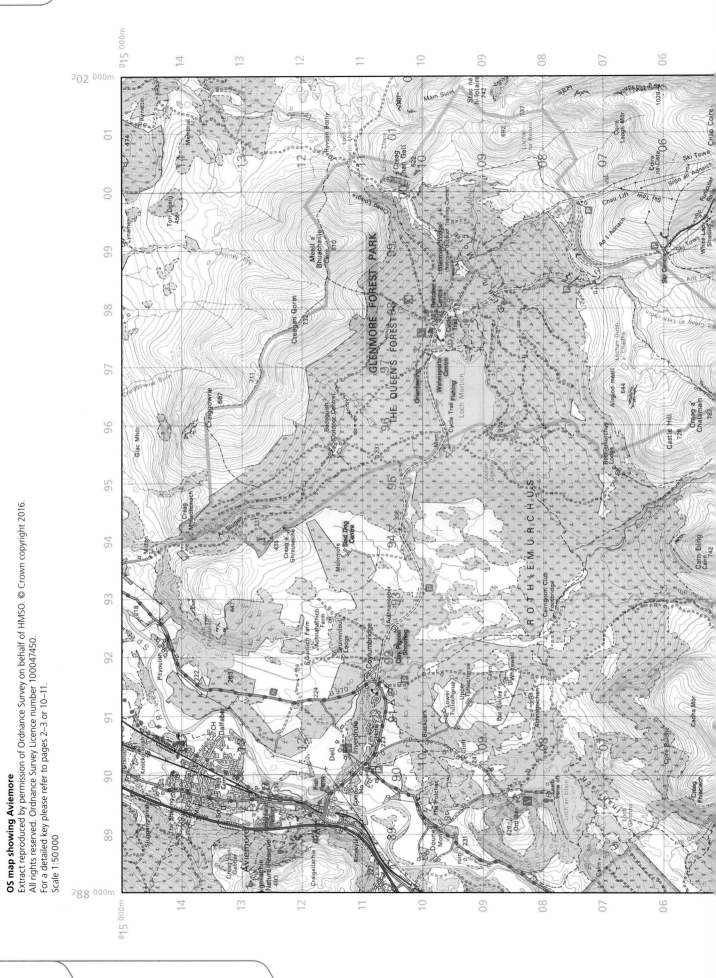

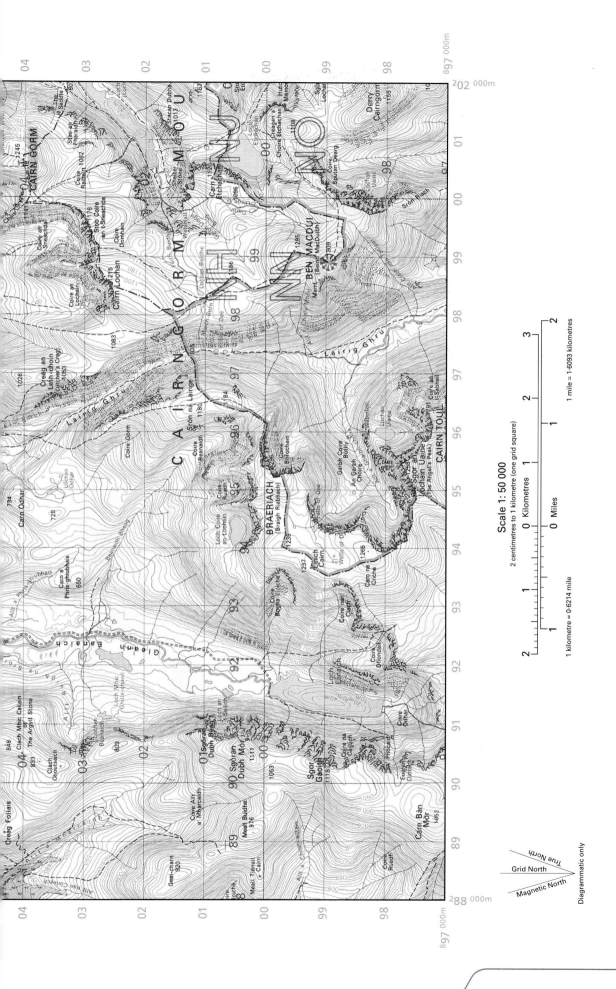

Scale 1: 50 000

2 centimetres to 1 kilometre (one grid square)

1 mile = 1·6093 kilometres

1 kilometre = 0·6214 mile

True North
Grid North
Magnetic North

Diagrammatic only

OS map showing Malham
Extract reproduced by permission of Ordnance Survey on behalf of HMSO. © Crown copyright 2016.
All rights reserved. Ordnance Survey Licence number 100047450.
For a detailed key please refer to pages 2–3 or 10–11.
Scale 1:50 000

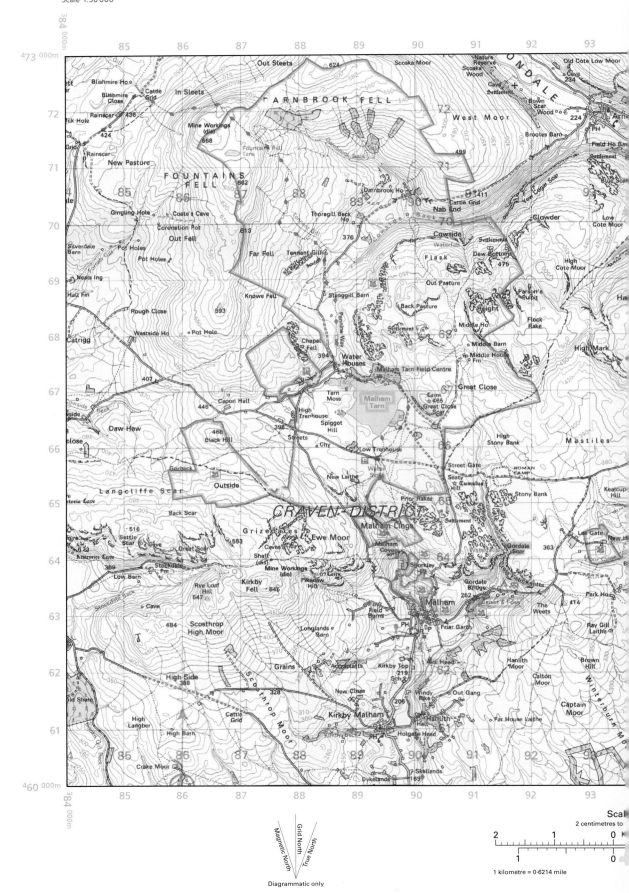

Scale
2 centimetres to

1 kilometre = 0·6214 mile

Magnetic North   Grid North   True North

Diagrammatic only

Duration: 1 hour, 45 minutes

Total marks: 60

SECTION 1 – PHYSICAL ENVIRONMENTS – 20 MARKS

Attempt EITHER question 1 OR question 2. ALSO attempt questions 3, 4 and 5.

SECTION 2 – HUMAN ENVIRONMENTS – 20 MARKS

Attempt questions 6, 7 and 8.

SECTION 3 – GLOBAL ISSUES – 20 MARKS

Attempt any TWO of the following:

Question 9 – Climate Change

Question 10 – Impact of Human Activity on the Natural Environment

Question 11 – Environmental Hazards

Question 12 – Trade and Globalisation

Question 13 – Tourism

Question 14 – Health

Remember, you can use sketches, maps and diagrams (labelled appropriately) in your answer, where relevant. Remember to identify which question you are answering in your answer booklet.

Section 1: Physical Environments

Total marks: 20

Attempt EITHER question 1 OR question 2 AND questions 3, 4 and 5.

Question 1   **Glaciated Uplands**

Study the Ordnance Survey map extract of the Aviemore area.

a) Match the glaciated upland features shown below with the correct grid reference.

Features – corrie, pyramidal peak, U-shaped valley

Choose from grid references:

954976

001981

917005

947020

3

HTP
Chapter 1.2
Page 10

b) **Explain** the formation of a U-shaped valley.
You may use a diagram(s) in your answer.

4

[Now answer questions 3, 4 and 5]

B

[Do not answer this question if you have already answered question 1]

Question 2   Upland Limestone

Study the Ordnance Survey map extract of the Malham area.

a) Match the limestone features shown below with the correct grid reference.

Features – limestone pavement, intermittent drainage, pot hole

Choose from grid references:

894657

900648

861681

853632

b) Explain the formation of a limestone pavement.

You may use a diagram(s) in your answer.

[Now answer questions 3, 4 and 5]

MARKS	STUDENT MARGIN
	HTP Chapter 1.2 Page 14
3	
4	

Question 3 Study the Ordnance Survey map extract of the Aviemore area.

The area of the map extract is popular with tourists.

Using **map evidence**, **explain** the attractions of the physical landscape for tourists.

MARKS

5

STUDENT MARGIN

HTP
Chapter 1.4
Page 21

Question 4   Diagram Q4: Average summer temperatures in the UK (Met Office)

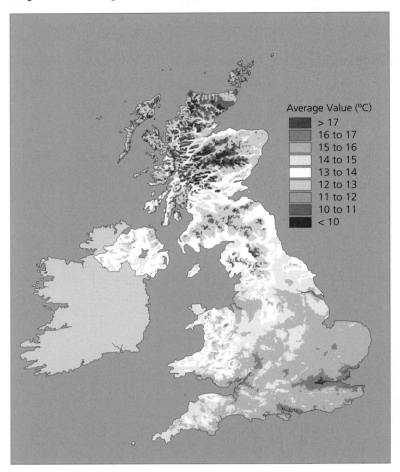

Average Value (°C)
> 17
16 to 17
15 to 16
14 to 15
13 to 14
12 to 13
11 to 12
10 to 11
< 10

Look at Diagram Q4.

Temperatures in London during the summer average around 17°C whereas in the north of Scotland temperatures average around 10°C.

Explain why factors like latitude, altitude, aspect and distance from the sea affect average UK temperatures.

4

HTP
Chapter 1.1
Page 2/3

MARKS | **STUDENT MARGIN**

Question 5   Diagram Q5: Synoptic chart, 26 February 2016

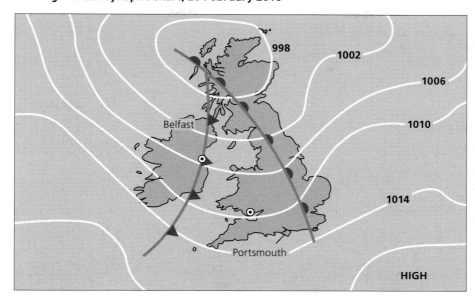

HTP
Chapter 1.1
Page 4/5

Study Diagram Q5.

'The yachting competition setting out from Belfast has been cancelled but Portsmouth's will go ahead.' (Facebook post)

Referring to the synoptic chart **explain** why this has happened.   4

[Now go to Section 2]

Section 2: Human Environments

Total marks: 20

Attempt questions 6, 7 and 8.

MARKS

Question 6   Diagram Q6: Proposed site of An Camas Mor (GR903115)

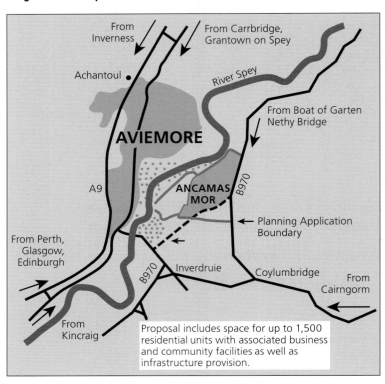

Study the Ordnance Survey map extract of the Aviemore area and Diagram Q6.

Find the site of An Camas Mor at 903115.

On the site at An Camas Mor it is proposed to build housing, businesses, community facilities and roads.

Using **map evidence**, give the advantages and disadvantages of this proposal.

5

Question 7   Diagram Q7: Population pyramids for China

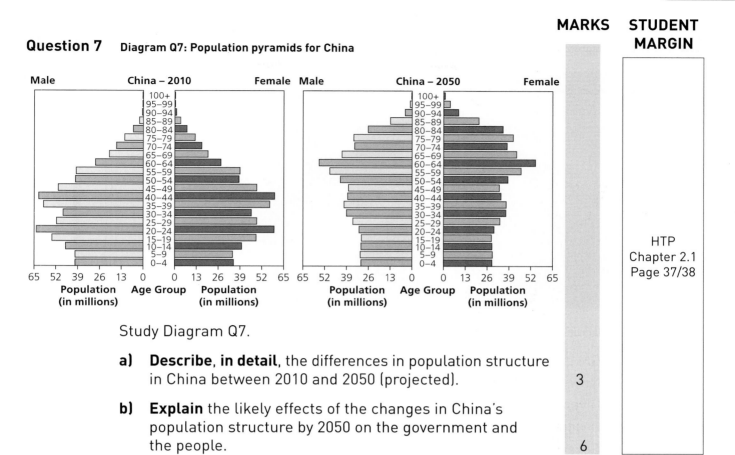

Study Diagram Q7.

a) **Describe**, **in detail**, the differences in population structure in China between 2010 and 2050 (projected).

3

b) **Explain** the likely effects of the changes in China's population structure by 2050 on the government and the people.

6

HTP
Chapter 2.1
Page 37/38

Question 8   Diagram Q8A: Modern milking parlour

Diagram Q8B: Selected farming developments

GM crops
New technology
Diversification
Organic farming
Government policy

Look at Diagrams Q8A and Q8B.

Choose **two** developments from Diagram Q8B.

Explain how your chosen developments affect farmers in the developed world.

[Now go to Section 3]

HTP
Chapter 2.3
Page 54/56

6

Section 3: Global Issues

Total marks: 20

Attempt any TWO questions.

Question 9 – Climate Change

Question 10 – Impact of Human Activity on the Natural Environment

Question 11 – Environmental Hazards

Question 12 - Trade and Globalisation

Question 13 – Tourism

Question 14 – Health

Question 9   Climate Change

MARKS

Diagram Q9A: Renewable energy produced by China and the USA

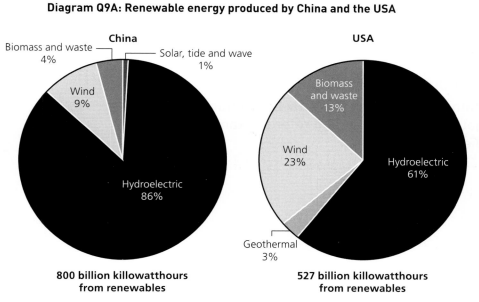

a)   Study Diagram Q9A.

Describe, **in detail**, the differences between renewable energy produced by China and the USA.

4

MARKS | **STUDENT MARGIN**

Diagram Q9B: Some effects of climate change

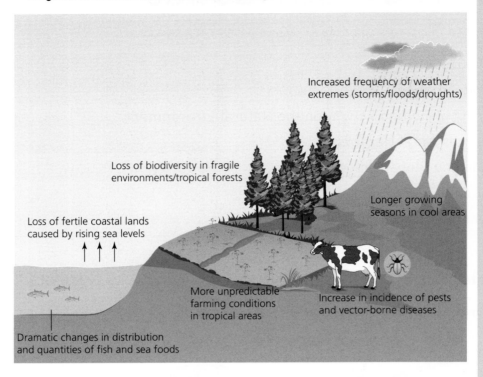

Increased frequency of weather extremes (storms/floods/droughts)

Loss of biodiversity in fragile environments/tropical forests

Longer growing seasons in cool areas

Loss of fertile coastal lands caused by rising sea levels

↑ ↑ ↑

More unpredictable farming conditions in tropical areas

Increase in incidence of pests and vector-borne diseases

Dramatic changes in distribution and quantities of fish and sea foods

HTP Chapter 3.1 Page 61

b) Look at Diagram Q9B.

Explain ways in which the activities of humans can cause climate change. You should refer to examples you have studied in your answer.

6

Question 10 Impact of Human Activity on the Natural Environment

Diagram Q10: Climate graphs of Barrow, Alaska and Eismitte, Greenland

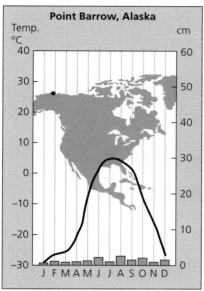

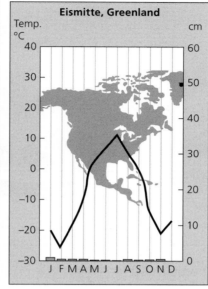

HTP
Chapter 3.2
Page 68/69

a) Study Diagram Q10.

Describe, **in detail**, the differences between the climate of Barrow and Eismitte.

4

b) Referring to examples you have studied, **explain** the advantages and disadvantages of removing tropical forests.

6

MARKS | STUDENT MARGIN

Question 11 Environmental Hazards

Diagram Q11A: Location of tropical storms

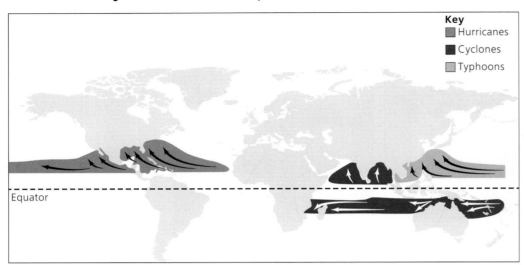

Key
- Hurricanes
- Cyclones
- Typhoons

Equator

a) Study Diagram Q11A.

Describe, **in detail**, the distribution of tropical storms.

4

Diagram Q11B: Satellite image of Hurricane Patricia, 23 October 2015

HTP
Chapter 3.3
Page 79

b) Look at Diagram Q11B.

'Hurricane Patricia, with 200 mph winds, was stronger than the deadliest and costliest hurricanes in history.'
(National Hurricane Center)

Explain the impact of a tropical storm on people and the environment. You must refer to named examples you have studied in your answer.

6

Question 12 Trade and Globalisation

Diagram Q12A: EU pattern of trade

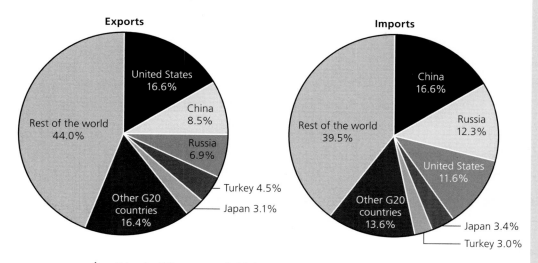

a) Study Diagram Q12A.

Describe, in detail, the pattern of trade in the EU.

4

Diagram Q12B: Fair trade

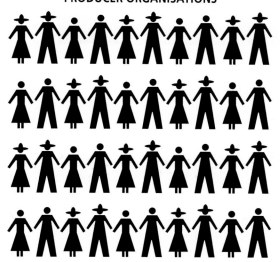

OVER
1.5 MILLION
FARMERS AND WORKERS
IN FAIRTRADE CERTIFIED
PRODUCER ORGANISATIONS

b) Look at Diagram Q12B.

Explain the benefits fair trade brings to people in developing countries.

6

HTP
Chapter 3.4
Page 84

Question 13 Tourism

Diagram Q13A: Visitor figures for selected UK National Parks

National Park name	Visitors per year (million)	Visitor days per year (million)	Visitor spend per year (million)
Brecon Beacons	4.15	5	£197
Cairngorms	1.5	3.1	£185
Lake District	16.4	24	£1,146
Dartmoor	2.4	3.1	£111

a) Study Diagram Q13A.

Describe, **in detail**, the differences in visitor figures for selected UK National Parks.

4

Diagram Q13B: Mass tourism

b) Look at Diagram Q13B.

Explain the growth of mass tourism.

6

HTP
Chapter 3.5
Page 87/88

Question 14 Health

Diagram Q14A: Percentage population at risk from malaria

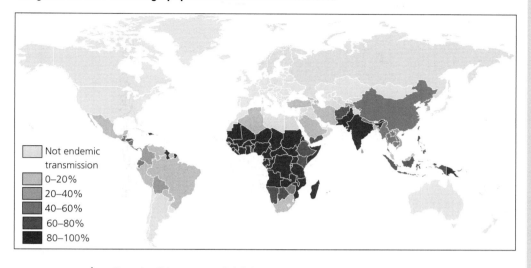

Not endemic transmission
0–20%
20–40%
40–60%
60–80%
80–100%

a) Study Diagram Q14A.

Describe, **in detail**, the distribution of areas at risk from malaria.

4

HTP
Chapter 3.6
Page 99

Diagram Q14B: Malaria life cycle

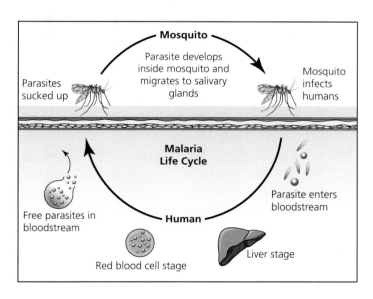

Mosquito

Parasite develops inside mosquito and migrates to salivary glands

Parasites sucked up

Mosquito infects humans

Malaria Life Cycle

Free parasites in bloodstream

Parasite enters bloodstream

Human

Red blood cell stage

Liver stage

b) Look at Diagram Q14B.

For **either** malaria, cholera, kwashiorkor **or** pneumonia **describe, in detail**, the effects on people.

6

[End of Practice Paper B]

National 5
Geography

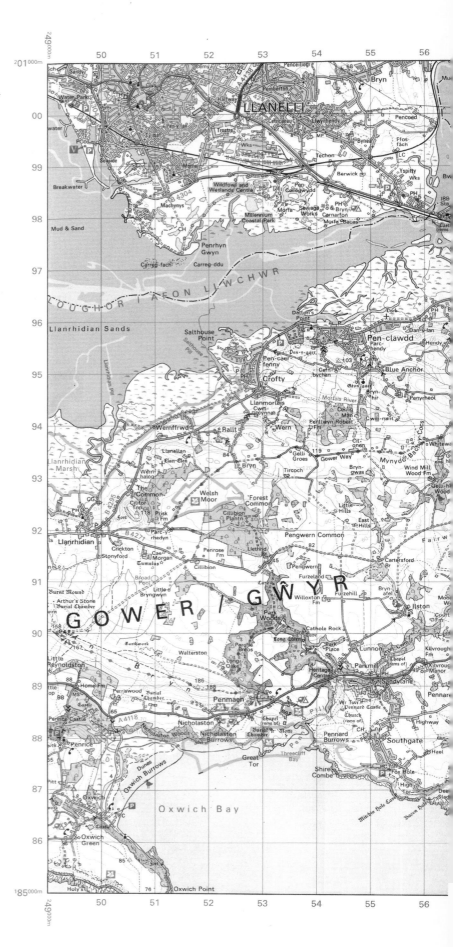

OS map showing Swansea

Extract reproduced by permission of Ordnance Survey on behalf of HMSO. © Crown copyright 2016. All rights reserved. Ordnance Survey Licence number 100047450.

For a detailed key please refer to pages 52–53.

Scale 1:50 000

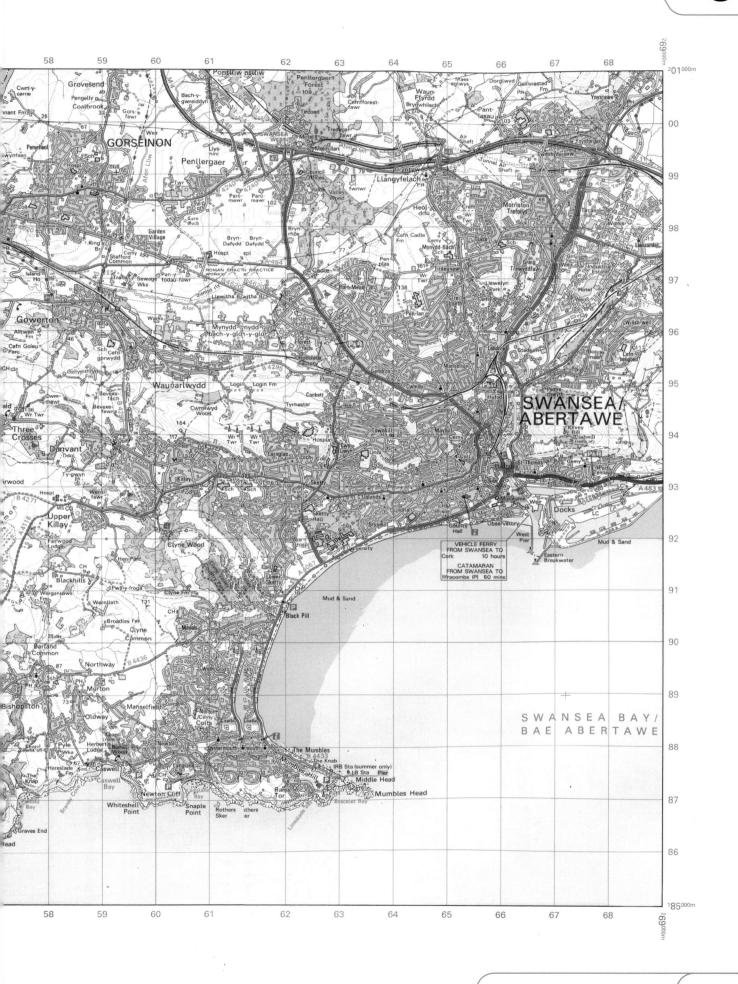

Duration: 1 hour, 45 minutes

Total marks: 60

SECTION 1 – PHYSICAL ENVIRONMENTS – 20 MARKS

Attempt EITHER question 1 OR question 2. ALSO attempt questions 3, 4 and 5.

SECTION 2 – HUMAN ENVIRONMENTS – 20 MARKS

Attempt questions 6, 7 and 8.

SECTION 3 – GLOBAL ISSUES – 20 MARKS

Attempt any TWO of the following:

Question 9 – Climate Change

Question 10 – Impact of Human Activity on the Natural Environment

Question 11 – Environmental Hazards

Question 12 – Trade and Globalisation

Question 13 – Tourism

Question 14 – Health

Remember, you can use sketches, maps and diagrams (labelled appropriately) in your answer, where relevant. Remember to identify which question you are answering in your answer booklet.

Section 1: Physical Environments

Total marks: 20

Attempt EITHER question 1 OR question 2 AND questions 3, 4 and 5.

	MARKS	STUDENT MARGIN

Question 1 **Coastal Landscapes**

Study the Ordnance Survey map extract of the Swansea area.

a) Match the coastal features shown below with the correct grid reference.

Features: headland, stack, bay

Choose from grid references:

612869

535877

570863

555869

	3	

b) **Explain** the formation of headlands and bays.

You may use a diagram(s) in your answer.

| | 4 | |

[Now answer questions 3, 4 and 5]

Student Margin: HTP Chapter 1.2 Page 12

C

[Do not answer this question if you have already answered question 1]

Question 2   Rivers and Valleys

Study the Ordnance Survey map extract of the East Kilbride area.

a) Match the river features shown below with the correct grid reference.
    Features: V-shaped valley, meander, waterfall
    Choose from grid references:

    591515

    684505

    652516

    575535   3

HTP
Chapter 1.2
Page 16

b) **Explain** the formation of a V-shaped valley.
    You may use a diagram(s) in your answer.   4

[Now answer questions 3, 4 and 5]

	MARKS	STUDENT MARGIN

Question 3   Study the Ordnance Survey map extract of the Swansea area.

Using **map evidence, explain** ways in which the physical landscape has affected land use on the map extract.

MARKS: 5

STUDENT MARGIN:
HTP
Chapter 1.3
Page 19/22

Question 4   Diagram Q4: Synoptic chart of the UK, 9 July 2015

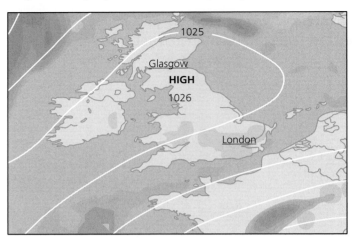

Look at Diagram Q4.

Explain the advantages and disadvantages brought about by an area of high pressure in summer to the UK.

4

HTP
Chapter 1.1
Page 5

Question 5   Diagram Q5: Landscape types and land uses in the UK

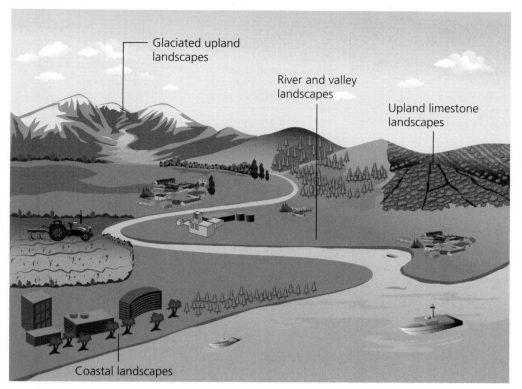

Glaciated upland
landscapes

River and valley
landscapes

Upland limestone
landscapes

Coastal landscapes

Land uses
- Farming
- Forestry
- Recreation and tourism
- Water storage and supply
- Renewable energy

Look at Diagram Q5.

Choose one landscape type you have studied from Diagram Q5.

Select **two** land uses from Diagram Q5 and **explain** why these land uses are in conflict with each other.

4

[Now go to Section 2]

HTP
Chapter 1.4
Page 25/27

OS map showing East Kilbride
Extract reproduced by permission of Ordnance Survey on behalf of HMSO. © Crown copyright 2016.
All rights reserved. Ordnance Survey Licence number 100047450.

ROADS AND PATHS

Not necessarily rights of way

Service area Junction number Elevated	
M1	Motorway (dual carriageway)
Unfenced	
A 470	Primary Route (recommended through route)
Dual carriageway	
A 493	Main road
Footbridge	
	Road under construction
B 4518	Secondary road
A 855 Bridge B 885	Narrow road with passing places
	Road generally more than 4m wide
	Road generally less than 4m wide
	Path / Other road, drive or track
	Gradient: steeper than 20% (1 in 5), 14% to 20% (1 in 7 to 1 in 5)
	Gates, Road tunnel
Ferry P Ferry V	Ferry (passenger), Ferry (vehicle)

RAILWAYS

Track multiple or single	Bridges, footbridge
Track under construction	Level crossing
Siding	Viaduct, embankment
Tunnel, cuttings	Station, (a) principal
Light rapid transit system, narrow gauge or tramway	Light rapid transit system station

WATER FEATURES

Marsh or salting Slopes Cliff Shingle
Towpath Lock Flat rock
Aqueduct Canal Ford Beacon Sand
Weir Lighthouse Lighthouse
Lake Footbridge Normal tidal limit (disused) (in use)
Bridge Dunes Low water mark
Canal (dry) Mud
High water mark

HEIGHTS

1 metre = 3·2808 feet

50	Contours are at 10 metres vertical interval
·144	Heights are to the nearest metre above mean sea level

Where two heights are shown the first height is to the base of the triangulation pillar and the second (in brackets) to the highest natural point of the hill

PUBLIC RIGHTS OF WAY

	Footpath
	Bridleway
	Restricted byway
	Byway open to all traffic

The symbols show the defined route so far as the scale of mapping will allow.

The representation on this map of any other road, track or path is no evidence of the existence of a right of way. Not shown on maps of Scotland

Danger Area Firing and Test Ranges in the area. Danger! Observe warning notices.

ROCK FEATURES

Outcrop Cliff
Scree

OTHER PUBLIC ACCESS

• • • •	Other route with public access (not normally shown in urban areas). Alignments are based on the best information available. These routes are not shown on maps of Scotland
● ●	On-road cycle route
○ ○	Traffic-free cycle route
4	National Cycle Network number
8	Regional Cycle Network number
◆ ◆	National Trail, European Long Distance Path, Long Distance Route, selected Recreational Routes

BOUNDARIES

—+—+—+—	National
—+·—+·—+·	District
—·—·—·—	County, Unitary Authority, Metropolitan District or London Borough
	National Park

ANTIQUITIES

+	Site of antiquity
⚔	Battlefield (with date)
☆ ····	Visible earthwork
VILLA	Roman
Castle	Non-Roman

TOURIST INFORMATION

	Camp site / caravan site
	Garden
	Golf course or links
i	Information centre (all year / seasonal)
	Nature reserve
P P&R	Parking, Park and ride (all year / seasonal)
✕	Picnic site
	Recreation / leisure / sports centre
	Selected places of tourist interest
✆	Telephone, public / roadside assistance
	Viewpoint
V	Visitor centre
!	Walks / Trails
	World Heritage site or area
▲	Youth hostel

LAND FEATURES

⟶	Electricity transmission line (pylons shown at standard spacing)
> – –> – –>	Pipe line (arrow indicates direction of flow)
ruin	Buildings
	Important building (selected)
	Bus or coach station
	Current or former place of worship { with tower / with spire, minaret or dome }
+	Place of worship
⌀	Glass structure
H	Heliport
△	Triangulation pillar
	Mast
	Wind pump, wind turbine
	Windmill with or without sails
+	Graticule intersection at 5' intervals
	Cutting, embankment
	Landfill site or slag/spoil heap
	Coniferous wood
	Non-coniferous wood
	Mixed wood
	Orchard
	Park or ornamental ground
	Forestry Commission land
	National Trust (always open / limited access, observe local signs)
	National Trust for Scotland (always open / limited access, observe local signs)

ABBREVIATIONS

Br	Bridge	MS	Milestone
Cemy	Cemetery	Mus	Museum
CG	Cattle grid	P	Post office
CH	Clubhouse	PC	Public convenience (in rural areas)
Fm	Farm	PH	Public house
Ho	House	Sch	School
MP	Milepost	TH	Town Hall, Guildhall or equivalent

Magnetic North Grid North True North

Diagrammatic only

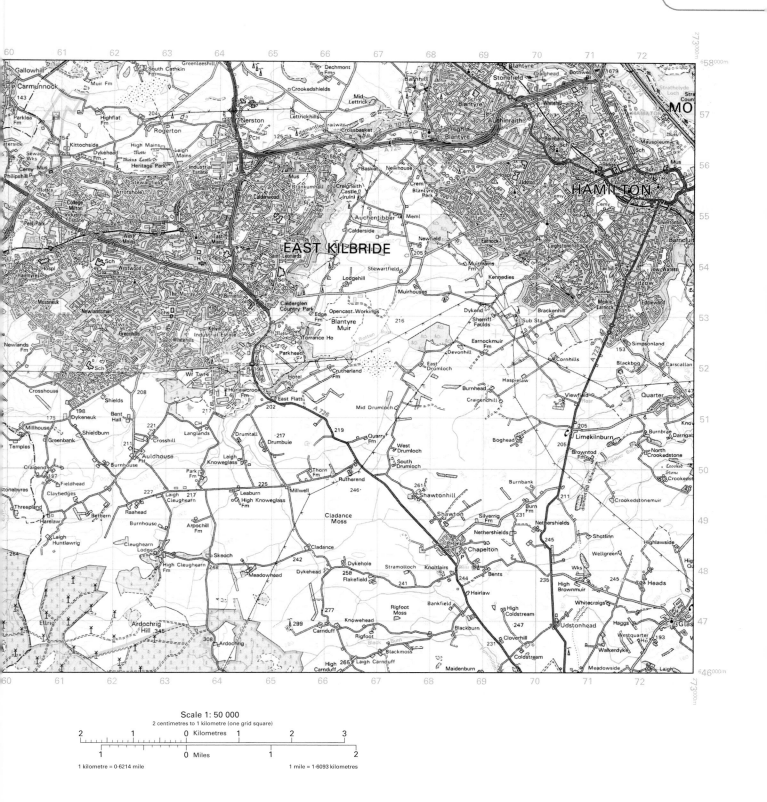

Scale 1: 50 000

2 centimetres to 1 kilometre (one grid square)

2   1   0   Kilometres   1   2   3

1   0   Miles   1   2

1 kilometre = 0·6214 mile   1 mile = 1·6093 kilometres

Section 2: Human Environments

Total marks: 20

Attempt questions 6, 7 and 8.

	MARKS	STUDENT MARGIN

Question 6   Study the Ordnance Survey map extract of the Hamilton/East Kilbride area.

a)   Give map evidence to show that the CBD of Hamilton is found in grid square 7255.

3

HTP
Chapter 2.2
Page 50

b)   East Kilbride has industrial estates found on the edge of the town, for example, Kelvin Industrial Estate at 640525.

Using **map evidence**, **explain** why these developments are found on the edge of town.

5

Question 7   Diagram Q7: Shanty town in Kolkata, India

Look at Diagram Q7.

For a named developing world city you have studied, **describe** methods used by city authorities to improve living conditions in shanty towns.

6

C

Question 8   **Diagram Q8: Demographic Transition Model**

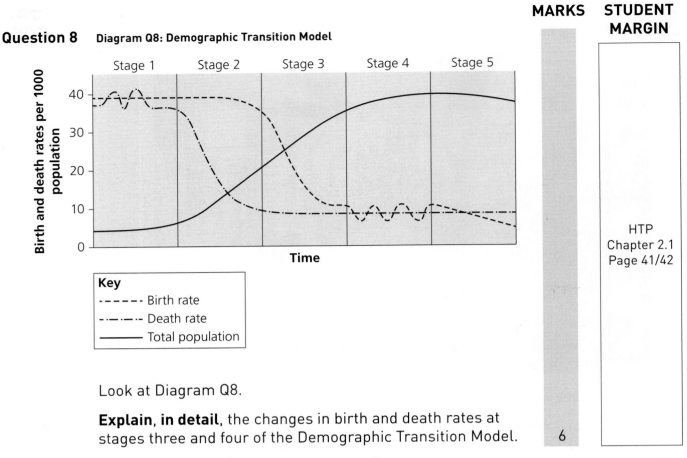

Look at Diagram Q8.

Explain, **in detail**, the changes in birth and death rates at stages three and four of the Demographic Transition Model.

[Now go to Section 3]

6

Section 3: Global Issues

Total marks: 20

Attempt any TWO questions.

Question 9 – Climate Change

Question 10 – Impact of Human Activity on the Natural Environment

Question 11 – Environmental Hazards

Question 12 – Trade and Globalisation

Question 13 – Tourism

Question 14 – Health

Question 9   Climate Change   MARKS   STUDENT MARGIN

Diagram Q9A: UK energy generation

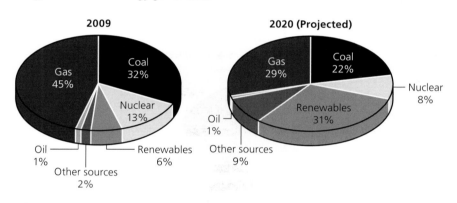

a)   Study Diagram Q9A.

Describe, **in detail**, the differences in energy generation between 2009 and 2020 (projected).   4

HTP Chapter 3.1 Page 61/62

Diagram Q9B: Paris Climate Change Summit 2015

b)   Look at Diagram Q9B.

Explain the local and global effects of climate change on people and the environment. You should refer to named examples you have studied in your answer.   6

C

Question 10 Impact of Human Activity on the Natural Environment

Diagram Q10A: Tree cover loss in the Brazilian Amazon 2001–2014

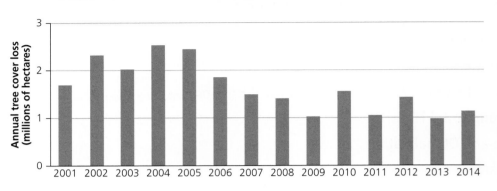

Study Diagram Q10A.

a) **Describe**, **in detail**, the tree cover loss in the Brazilian Amazon, 2001–2014.

4

Diagram Q10B: Land use in the rainforest

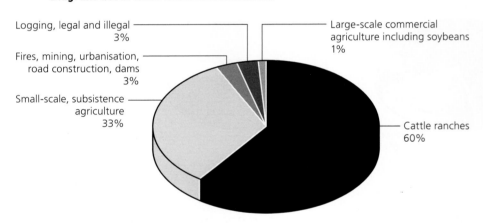

Logging, legal and illegal
3%

Fires, mining, urbanisation,
road construction, dams
3%

Small-scale, subsistence
agriculture
33%

Large-scale commercial
agriculture including soybeans
1%

Cattle ranches
60%

HTP
Chapter 3.2
Page 68/69

b) Look at Diagram Q10B.

Choose **two** land uses from Diagram Q10B.
Explain how **your chosen land uses** can lead to degradation of the rainforest.

6

Question 11 Environmental Hazards

Diagram Q11A: Distribution of earthquakes and volcanoes

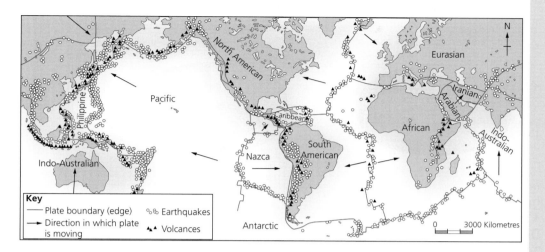

a) Study Diagram Q11A.

Describe, **in detail**, the distribution of earthquakes.

Diagram Q11B: Selected natural disasters

b) Look at Diagram Q11B.

For a named environmental hazard you have studied, **explain** methods used to predict and plan for its occurrence.

4

6

HTP
Chapter 3.3
Page 79

Question 12 Trade and Globalisation

Diagram Q12A: Share of world GDP

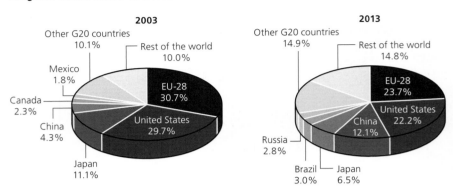

a) Study Diagram Q12A.

Describe, **in detail**, the changes in global exports between 2006 and 2014.

4

HTP
Chapter 3.4
Page 82

Diagram Q12B: Exports of a developing country

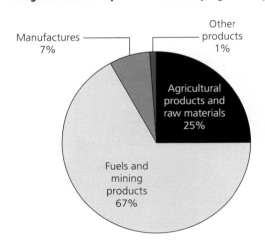

b) Look at Diagram Q12B.

Many developing countries rely on one product to export. **Explain** the effects changing demand for the product will have on the country.

6

MARKS | STUDENT MARGIN

Question 13 Tourism

Diagram Q13A: International tourist arrivals by destination 2010–2030 (projected)

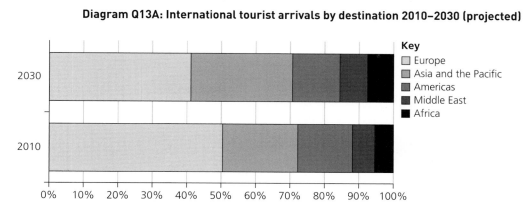

Key
- ☐ Europe
- ☐ Asia and the Pacific
- ▨ Americas
- ▨ Middle East
- ■ Africa

a) Study Diagram Q13A.

Describe, **in detail**, the projected changes in international tourist arrivals 2010–2030.

4

HTP
Chapter 3.5
Page 88/89

Diagram Q13B: Ecotourism

eco TOURISM

b) Look at Diagram Q13B.

Explain the advantages ecotourism brings to the people and environment of a developing country.

You should refer to an area you have studied in your answer.

6

MARKS | **STUDENT MARGIN**

Question 14 Health

Diagram Q14A: Presence of obesity (%) in men over the age of 18, 2014

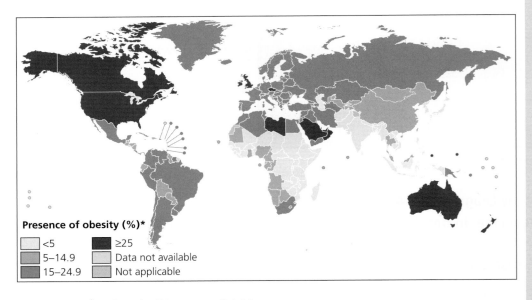

Presence of obesity (%)*

<5	≥25
5–14.9	Data not available
15–24.9	Not applicable

a) Study Diagram Q14A.

Describe, **in detail**, the world distribution of obesity in men over the age of 18.

4

HTP
Chapter 3.6
Page 97/98

Diagram Q14B: Selected health facts 2016

- Every seven minutes someone in the UK will have a heart attack

- Globally smoking causes 71% of lung cancers

- In the UK 37% of men and 28% of women regularly exceed the government's recommendations for alcohol

b) Look at Diagram Q14B.

For **either** heart disease, cancer **or** asthma, **explain** the main causes of your chosen disease.

6

[End of Practice Paper C]

National 5
Geography

Practice Paper A

Section 1: Physical Environments

1 **a)** **Hint:** First match the features you are sure are correct. You can then match any remaining feature to its reference. Do not leave a feature without a reference. Even if you do not know the correct answer take a guess at the remaining references as you could be lucky and match it correctly!

Truncated spur: 476683

Corrie: 467677

U-shaped valley: 525594 **3 marks**

b) **Hint:** The more detail you put into an answer the more marks you will gain. If you simply refer to glacial processes like plucking, abrasion and freeze-thaw you will gain only 1 mark. However, you will gain additional marks if you explain the processes. You can gain a mark for drawing a series of diagrams which shows how the feature is formed at different stages. A diagram with labels which explain the formation can gain full marks.

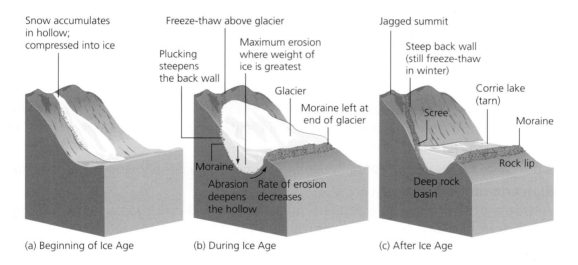

(a) Beginning of Ice Age   (b) During Ice Age   (c) After Ice Age

Snow accumulates in a north facing hollow in a mountainside where the snow becomes compacted and turns into ice **(1)**; the glacier moves downhill due to gravity **(1)**. Plucking occurs on the back wall, making it steeper **(1)**. The ice sticks to the sides and pulls pieces of rock away as it moves **(1)**. Abrasion deepens the bottom of the hollow **(1)** as rock fragments embedded in the bottom of the glacier act like sandpaper, wearing away the land **(1)**. When temperatures rose at the end of the Ice Age the glacier melted, leaving behind an armchair-shaped hollow with steep sides **(1)**. A rock lip forms at the edge of the hollow and water becomes trapped, creating a corrie loch or tarn **(1)**. **4 marks**

2   **a)   Hint:** Match the features you are sure are correct. You can then match the remaining feature to its reference. Do not leave a feature without a reference. Even if you do not know the correct answer take a guess at the remaining references as you could be lucky and match it correctly!

V-shaped valley: 473657

Meander: 447585

Tributary: 528595   **3 marks**

b)   Hint: The more detail you put into an answer the more marks you will gain. If you simply refer to river processes like hydraulic action, attrition, corrosion and corrasion you will gain only 1 mark. However, you will gain additional marks if you explain the processes. You can gain a mark for drawing a series of diagrams which shows how the feature is formed at different stages. A diagram with labels which explains the formation can gain full marks.

Waterfalls are found where hard rock like limestone overlies softer rock like mudstone **(1)**. The water is powerful and erodes the softer rock by hydraulic action **(1)**. This is the force of the water hitting off the rock **(1)**. Through time a plunge pool forms **(1)**. The softer rock is worn away and the hard rock is undercut **(1)** and an overhang of hard rock is left suspended above the plunge pool **(1)**. This collapses as there is nothing to support it and the rock falls into the plunge pool **(1)**. Rock fragments swirling around deepen the plunge pool **(1)**. This process is repeated over a long period of time and the waterfall retreats upstream forming a steep-sided gorge **(1)**.   **4 marks**

3   **Hint:** Make sure you read the question. This question is asking you to explain why the area in the map extract is suitable for your chosen land use. This means you must give reasons in your answer. Your answer must refer to map evidence. Giving an appropriate grid reference (preferably a six figure grid reference) will gain you a mark. Do not list the type of activities that you identify on the map – this is simple description. For example: 'The area can be used to ski, climb, sail, etc.' What you should say is: 'There are mountains in the area which have steep slopes which are good for skiing.' Name the feature on the map, then give the reason why it is good for your chosen land use.

Examples are given for four different land uses. You would only need to answer on one land use.

If recreation and tourism chosen:

There is a variety of scenery, e.g. glaciated mountains, rivers and coasts **(1)** attracting a range of visitors from sightseers to photographers **(1)**. There are mountains which can be used for climbing and walking **(1)**. Water activities like sailing or wind surfing are possible in the surrounding rivers and lochs, for example Loch Garve **(1)** at 412592 **(1)**. There are forested areas which can be used for walking, bird watching, picnicking, for example at 481611 **(1)**. Flat land near the coast is suitable for tourist accommodation in the form of caravan/camp sites **(1)**.   **5 marks**

Forestry (e.g. 4763)

Large parts of the map area are very steep and would be unsuitable for most other land uses **(1)**. Many of the slopes are too steep to use machinery **(1)**. Much of the land is high and too cold for crops to grow **(1)**. Soils might be acidic and rainfall is likely to be high, but coniferous trees can grow in these conditions **(1)** and there is access via the A834 to transport the logs to market **(1)**.

Farming (e.g. 5164)

The land is above 400m so hill sheep farming would be possible here as the animals can manage on the steep slopes **(1)**. Valley bottoms could be used for mixed farming like Knockbain at 523587 as the climate is warmer and the land flatter **(1)**.

Water storage and supply (e.g. 4162)
The glaciated uplands of the map contain lochs like Loch an Tuirc and Loch na Gearra **(1)**
These could be used to store water and to supply water to towns like Dingwall **(1)**. These
areas are high up and tend to have high rainfall to feed the supply **(1)**.

4 **Hint:** Make sure you refer to a specific area you have studied. Sometimes marks can be lost if
you give a general answer. Marks will not be given for describing the land use conflicts – you
must give strategies to solve the conflicts. Remember, if the question is worth 4 marks you need
to make four points to get the marks. Examples are given for coastal landscapes and glaciated
upland landscapes. You only need to answer on one landscape.

Glaciated upland areas
If the Lake District chosen:
Areas like the Lake District and Loch Lomond are designated as National Parks so the
landscape is protected by law **(1)**. To prevent traffic congestion in the small villages and to
prevent inconsiderate parking the number of car parks have been increased **(1)**. In some
areas Park and Ride schemes have been created to reduce the amount of traffic on the small
country roads as well as the villages themselves **(1)**. Bodies such as the National Parks
Authority try to educate the public through the use of leaflets, presentations and well informed
Park Rangers to talk to the visitors **(2)**. Information boards at important sites and car parks
give specific details about a site and advice on access **(2)**. Construction of ladder stiles over
walls and step stiles through fences where rights of way cross field boundaries prevents
these getting destroyed by walkers etc. **(2)**. Visitors are encouraged by signposts to keep to the
public footpaths to reduce footpath erosion **(1)**. Notices are put up during lambing time to ask
visitors to be especially considerate of farmers' needs e.g. keep dogs on the lead **(2)**. Building
in these areas is controlled and permission has to be given for any new structures **(1)**.

Costal landscpes
If the Dorset coast chosen:
The Dorset coast has been designated a World Heritage Site, allowing local authorities to
protect the coast from over-development with strict planning controls **(1)**. Recreational
activities like boating, yachting, fishing, etc., take place in Poole harbour so zoning of
areas ensures that different activities are kept apart **(1)**. Speed limits have also been put
in place reducing the danger to other users as well as reducing the erosional effects on
the shoreline **(2)**. Additional parking and alternative types of transport like train lines and
new bus routes have been introduced to reduce traffic congestion and pollution **( )**. Nature
reserves have been created to protect local wildlife to try to reduce the impact of tourists
using the beaches **(1)**. Fines have been introduced to deter people from dropping litter **(1)**.
Rangers are employed to prevent problems and educate visitors **(1)**.   **4 marks**

5 **Hint:** Before you start to answer a weather question with a synoptic chart you must always
check the date of the chart. The weather will be different depending on the time of year,
especially for an anticyclone. Do not describe the weather or list the weather – this will gain
you very few marks. You need to interpret the chart to give reasons for the weather being
experienced.

The Mediterranean has an area of high pressure over it and high pressure systems bring
settled weather lasting for a period of time **(1)**. Conditions are clear as high pressure in
summer brings limited cloud cover **(1)**. There are no fronts over the area so no rainfall **(1)**.
The isobars are far apart so there are gentle winds **(1)**. The temperature is high which is
typical of high pressure in this area in the summer **(1)**. The UK is experiencing a depression
which brings changeable weather **(1)**. Depressions bring clouds, causing overcast
conditions **(1)**. There is a front close to the NW of the UK which will bring rain **(1)**. Winds will
be strong as the isobars are close together **(1)**.   **4 marks**

Section 2: Human Environments

6 **Hint:** For full marks you must refer to both areas. You must use map evidence in your answer. Refer to specific examples from the map. You may gain a mark from giving an appropriate grid reference.

Area A: The Suburbs

The suburbs are located closer to the edge of Preston so have been built more recently **(1)**. There is more open space than in the CBD which is in the centre of town **(1)**. The patterns of the streets are curvilinear with cul-de-sacs **(1)** as shown at grid reference 524328 **(1)**. There are amenities like a hospital, leisure centre and several schools provided for the residents **(1)**.

Area B: The Central Business District

This is the CBD as it's in the centre of the town **(1)**. The main transport routes meet here **(1)**. It has a main railway station at 536290 **(1)**. There is a tourist information centre **(1)** and a museum **(1)**. There are many churches, indicating that it is the oldest part of town **(1)**.   **5 marks**

7 **a)** **Hint:** In this question you must use figures to gain full marks. General statements like higher or lower/increasing or decreasing might only gain you 2 marks. Try to process the information. Instead of saying the UK has a higher life expectancy at 81 than Chad at only 51 you could say: 'In the UK people are expected to live until they are 81 which is 30 years more than in Chad.'

The UK has a far greater GNP by $36,174 **(1)**. The UK has a literacy rate of 99% which is 52% higher than Chad's **(1)**. Only 22% of the population of Chad are employed outside agriculture whereas in the UK this figure is 99% **(1)**. People in Chad are expected to live for 30 years less than in the UK **(1)**. There are far more people per doctor in Chad than there are in the UK **(1)** – by 19,600 **(1)**.   **3 marks**

    b) **Hint:** You are asked to choose two indicators. Do not talk about all the indicators as you will only gain marks for two of them. You need to give detail to gain the marks. Remember, you need to explain why there is a difference between the UK and Chad.

If Life expectancy chosen:

Countries with a high life expectancy like the UK have the money to invest in health care **(1)**. They have hospitals and modern technology and drugs to keep people healthier **(1)**. Jobs are less strenuous and less dangerous which improves life expectancy **(1)**. Money is invested in the elderly, resulting in better life expectancy **(1)**.

If % employed in agriculture chosen:

Countries like the UK have a low percentage employed in agriculture as they have money available to invest in industry **(1)** so more people are employed in industry which means people have a higher standard of living **(1)** due to higher wages **(1)**. Countries with a low percentage employed in agriculture can afford to import food from other countries rather than grow it all themselves **(1)**.   **6 marks**

8 **Hint:** In this question be careful not to simply describe the features of the rural/urban fringe. The question asks for reasons so take each feature and say why it attracts businesses to that area. For example, 'feature – flat land, reason – easy to build on'. Sometimes this question is asked as a map question. In that case you need to give specific examples from the map. For example, if you say there is good access into the area, give the actual road number (e.g. M25) from the map. This shows the examiner your skills in interpreting a map.

They are attracted to this area as it is located outside town which means there is plenty of parking space **(1)**. This is needed as many customers arrive by car **(1)**. These are large developments and take up a lot of space which is available on the rural/urban fringe **(1)**. The land on the outside of town is cheaper **(1)**. The cheaper land allows the houses to be bigger with cul-de-sacs, gardens, etc. **(1)**. The houses can provide a source of labour and customers for the airport and the business park **(1)**. There is less congestion away from the CBD allowing easy access for receiving/delivery of goods **(1)**.   **6 marks**

Section 3: Global Issues

9   **a)**   **Hint:** In this question you must use figures to gain full marks. General statements like higher or lower/increasing or decreasing might only gain you 2 marks. Try to process the information in some way. Since the question asks about changes you would gain no marks for mentioning transport as there is no change in this category.

Overall greenhouse gas emissions have increased over the last 20 years **(1)**. However, there has been a decrease in both agriculture and buildings **(1)**. The largest decrease was agriculture which dropped from 27% to 21%, a difference of 6% **(1)**. Emissions have increased in industry by 2% from 19% to 21% **(1)**. Energy emissions have increased the greatest from 32% to 37%, a rise of 5% **(1)**. Emissions from buildings have shown a small decrease of 1% **(1)**.   **4 marks**

b)   **Hint:** In this question you need to give ways to manage climate change. You should put as much detail into your answer as possible. A simple list of methods will gain you only a few marks. Remember, this question is worth 6 marks so you need to make at least six valid points to get all the marks.

Laws can be introduced to reduce the burning of forests, thus reducing the amount of CO_2 going into the atmosphere **(1)**. Introducing replanting schemes where forests have been destroyed can reduce the amount of CO_2 in the atmosphere **(1)**. The use of sprays which include CFCs can be reduced as CFCs pollute the atmosphere **(1)**. Council bylaws can be put in place to prevent illegal disposal of fridges, etc., so that no CFCs are allowed to escape **(1)** as well as introducing controlled disposal on waste dumping sites **(1)**. Exhaust emissions containing lead and carbon dioxide can be reduced by adding filter systems to vehicle exhaust systems **(1)** and cars/lorries can be produced which use lead free fuel **(1)**. We can reduce the use of fossil fuels such as coal, oil and natural gases by introducing green friendly fuels such as HEP, wind power, solar power and other renewable energy sources **(1)**.   **6 marks**

10   **a)**   **Hint:** In this question you must use figures and dates to gain full marks. General statements like higher or lower/increasing or decreasing might only gain you 2 marks. Try to process the information in some way. Marks can be awarded for overall trends.

Overall the percentage ice coverage has increased from 70% in 2000 to 92% in 2015 **(1)**. Ice coverage increased slowly between 2000 and 2002, increasing by 3% **(1)**. It then dropped between 2002 and 2006 from 73% to 53%, a difference of 20% **(1)**. The biggest drop was between 2009 and 2010 where it fell by 35% **(1)**. It rose again between 2010 and 2012 reaching 89% in 2012 **(1)**. It fell again in 2013 before reaching its highest point in 2015 at around 92% **(1)**.   **4 marks**

b) **Hint:** To gain full marks for this question you need to mention both the people and the environment. Remember that you can mention both positive and negative effects in your answer. You should refer to specific case studies in your answer. Remember, the more detail in your answer the more marks you can achieve. A list of effects will gain you only 1 mark. If you describe instead of explaining you may get no marks at all.

If the rainforest chosen:
In Brazil large areas have been cleared by timber companies and the hardwood has been exported abroad, earning income for the country **(1)** as well as providing jobs for the locals **(1)**. Forests are cleared for new farmland, settlement and to increase food production so destroying the habitats of wildlife **(1)**. Burning trees releases vast quantities of carbon dioxide into the atmosphere and may contribute to global warming **(1)**. The homes of indigenous tribes are destroyed, as is their traditional culture and way of life **(1)**, and the people catch diseases from new settlers, causing many to die **(1)**. Plants which may contain cures for diseases are also destroyed **(1)**. When the trees have been cleared, there is less protection for the soil and heavy rain can lead to rapid soil erosion **(1)**. Minerals are leached out of the soil and the soil quickly becomes infertile and useless **(1)**. Poor farmers lose their land and may be forced to migrate to towns and cities to find employment, resulting in an increase in shanty towns **(1)**.

If the Tundra chosen:
The discovery of oil in Alaska resulted in the building of the Trans-Alaskan pipeline that caused damage to the Tundra vegetation and wildlife **(1)**. The pipeline disrupts the habitat of the caribou diverting them from their natural hunting areas and migration routes **(1)**. Burst pipes have spilled hundreds of thousands of gallons of crude oil in Alaska, devastating the fragile environment **(1)**. Oil spills from tankers like the Exxon Valdez have also been responsible for pollution in the region as well as causing the deaths of multitudes of birds and sea creatures **(1)**. Local Inuit people have had their way of life disrupted as they must detour around the pipeline **(1)** and may no longer have access to their traditional hunting grounds **(1)**. Some jobs were created by the oil industry but few jobs are available for locals and those which are, are poorly paid **(1)**. Roads are built to transport workers and machinery further damaging the vegetation and environment as well as creating air and noise pollution **(1)**. The roads, however, improve access for the local people **(1)**.
6 marks

11 a) **Hint:** Remember the map is there to help you answer the question. Try to name areas or countries in your answer. There are no marks for explanation, only for description, so do not explain your answer. Do not list places as this will gain you only 1 mark.

Active volcanoes are found along the edges of the plate boundaries **(1)**. There is a large concentration around the Pacific Ring of Fire **(1)**. There are a large number down the west coast of the USA and Alaska **(1)**. The majority of volcanoes in South America are found down the west coast, for example Chile **(1)**. Europe has few volcanoes with most found around southern Europe, for example Mount Etna in Sicily **(1)**. Any volcanoes in Africa are found on the eastern side of the continent with concentrations like the East African Rift Valley **(1)**.
4 marks

b) **Hint:** Do not list the strategies as this will gain you only 1 mark. The question asks for explanation so you must give reasons in your answer. State the strategy, then say why it reduces the effects. Avoid describing. You need to refer to an example you have studied otherwise you may lose a mark.

If the Japanese earthquake 2011 chosen:

People living in earthquake prone areas like Japan have emergency plans in place so that they know exactly what to do during an earthquake **(1)**. Emergency supplies such as bottled water and tinned food are stockpiled to ensure they have vital supplies to survive in the event of an earthquake **(1)**. In Japanese schools earthquake drills are held so that children know what to do in the event of an earthquake **(1)**. Earthquake-resistant buildings reduce the number of people trapped or killed as the buildings are designed to twist and sway instead of collapsing **(1)**. Sprinkler systems and gas cut-off valves prevent fires spreading, reducing the number of people injured and buildings destroyed **(1)**. The government sends texts and issues warnings on TV giving the people some warning to evacuate or take cover **(1)**. The government has plans in place to allow aid to be quickly sent to an affected area, thus reducing the number of injured **(1)**.
6 marks

12 a) Hint: In this question you must use figures and dates to gain full marks. General statements like higher or lower/increasing or decreasing might only gain you 2 marks. Try to process the information in some way. Marks can be awarded for overall trends.

Overall the percentage volume of world trade has decreased since 2008 **(1)**. It dropped steeply between 2008 and 2009 from +6% to -18% **(1)**, a drop of 24% **(1)**. It then rose steeply between 2009 and 2010 from -18% to +19% **(1)**, an increase of 37% **(1)**. It reached its highest point in 2010 at +19% **(1)**. It then steadily decreased till 2013 where it remained relatively steady till 2014 **(1)**. It continued to drop to around 1% in 2015 **(1)**.
4 marks

b) Hint: You should try to give examples in your answer. In some cases, if you do not give an example or refer to a case study, you can lose a mark. Remember, this is an explanation question so you need to give reasons in your answer.

Developed countries have a larger share of world trade because their exports include much more manufactured goods than countries in the developing world **(1)**. Developing countries tend to produce raw materials rather than manufactured goods **(1)** and manufactured goods sell for more than raw materials **(1)**. Developed countries have more industries producing a wide variety of products which are traded with other developed countries **(1)**. Many developed countries like Germany belong to trading alliances such as the European Union which help to increase the volume of trade **(1)**. The economies of developed countries benefit from being able to purchase low cost raw materials produced by developing countries and sell manufactured goods back for higher profits **(1)**. Developing countries like Chad have much less money to invest in manufacturing industries and are less able to compete with developed countries **(1)**.
6 marks

13 a) Hint: In this question you must use figures and dates to gain full marks. General statements like higher or lower/increasing or decreasing might only gain you 2 marks. Try to process the information in some way. Marks can be awarded for overall trends.

International tourist arrivals have increased in all these areas **(1)**. The greatest increase is in Asia and the Pacific which has more than quadrupled **(1)** increasing by 209 million in 24 years **(1)**. Europe has more than doubled **(1)** increasing from 250 million in 1990 to 575 million in 2014, an increase of 325 million **(1)**. The Americas have nearly doubled from 99 million to 189 million, an increase of 90 million **(1)**. In 2009 all three areas saw a decrease in arrivals **(1)** with Europe decreasing by 31 million **(1)**.
4 marks

b) **Hint:** For full marks you need to mention both the people and the environment. You should refer to examples you have studied. The question asks for the impact of mass tourism. Remember, that means you can mention both advantages and disadvantages in your answer.

In Mallorca mass tourism creates employment for the local people in shops, hotels, restaurants, car hire, etc. **(1)**. It decreases unemployment and increases the standards of living **(1)**. The income from tourism allows the government to improve infrastructure, e.g. transport, water supplies and sewage systems **(1)**. The facilities provided for the tourists can be used by the locals, improving their access to sports facilities, clubs and water parks **(1)**. An increased demand for food to supply hotels, restaurants and cafes provides farmers with a larger market for their produce, increasing their profit **(1)**. However, employment can be seasonal as many hotels in resorts like Pollensa close at the end of October **(1)**. Traditional ways of life can be lost as young people leave the countryside to live and work in the tourist resorts rather than family farms **(2)**. Tourism creates pollution, e.g. litter on beaches **(1)**. Increased traffic causes noise and air pollution as well as traffic congestion in local villages **(2)**. Large numbers of tourists visiting natural features like limestone caves can damage the delicate structures **(1)**. Beaches are eroded as sand is carried away on tourists' feet **(1)**. Large areas of natural grassland/forest are removed to make way for new hotels, etc. **(1)**, destroying the natural habitat of plants and animals **(1)**.   **6 marks**

14 **a)** **Hint:** Remember, the map is there for you to answer the question. Try to name areas or countries in your answer, as well as referring to percentages. There are no marks for explanation, only for description, so do not explain your answer. Do not list places as this will gain you only 1 mark.

Areas like North America, Australasia and Europe have health care access of over 95% **(1)**. The area with the least health care access is Africa with many countries having less than 20% **(1)**. The only country in southern Africa with health care access over 95% is South Africa **(1)**. Most African countries which border the Mediterranean Sea have over 50% health care with Libya having over 95% **(1)**. The only country in Africa bordering the Mediterranean which has less is Morocco at between 20% and 49% **(1)**. Most of South America has over 50% health care access apart from Paraguay, Bolivia and Ecuador **(1)**. India is the main area in Asia with less than 20% **(1)**.   **4 marks**

b) **Hint:** Do not simply list the strategies. You should add as much detail to your answer as possible. Refer to examples if you can.

Health Education programmes have been introduced to limit the spread of AIDS/HIV in developing and developed countries **(1)** promoting the benefits of safe sex and the dangers of sharing hypodermic needles **(1)**. Antiretroviral drugs which work by stopping the virus replicating in the body, allowing the immune system to repair itself and preventing further damage, are more freely available **(1)**. Condoms are available for free **(1)** and TV and radio advertising has been used to inform the public **(1)**. Agencies such as the World Bank have made funding available to developing countries to tackle the disease **(1)**. In developed countries, needle exchanges and drug therapy programmes have been introduced **(1)**.   **6 marks**

Practice Paper B

Section 1: Physical Environments

1 a) **Hint:** First match the features you are sure are correct. You can then match any remaining feature to its reference. Do not leave a feature without a reference. Even if you do not know the correct answer take a guess at the remaining references as you could be lucky and match it correctly!

Corrie: 001981

Pyramidal peak: 954976

U-shaped valley: 917005 **3 marks**

b) **Hint:** The more detail you put into an answer the more marks you will gain. If you simply refer to glacial processes like plucking, abrasion and freeze-thaw you will gain only 1 mark. However, you will gain additional marks if you explain the processes. You can gain a mark for drawing a series of diagrams which shows how the feature is formed at different stages. A diagram with labels which explain the formation can gain full marks.

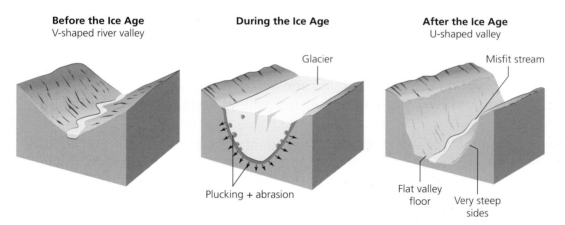

Before the Ice Age
V-shaped river valley

During the Ice Age
Glacier
Plucking + abrasion

After the Ice Age
U-shaped valley
Misfit stream
Flat valley floor
Very steep sides

A glacier moves down a main valley which it erodes by plucking **(1)**, where the ice freezes onto fragments of rock and pulls them away **(1)**, and abrasion, where rock fragments embedded in the ice scrape the land surface **(1)**. The weight and erosive power of the glacier remove interlocking spurs **(1)**. As a result the valley becomes deeper, straighter and wider **(1)**. **4 marks**

2 a) **Hint:** First match the features you are sure are correct. You can then match any remaining feature to its reference. Do not leave a feature without a reference. Even if you do not know the correct answer take a guess at the remaining references as you could be lucky and match it correctly!

Limestone pavement: 900648

Intermittent drainage: 894657

Pot hole: 861681 **3 marks**

b) **Hint:** The more detail you put into an answer the more marks you will gain. You should mention processes in your answer. You can gain a mark for drawing a series of diagrams which shows how the feature is formed at different stages. A diagram with labels which explain the formation can gain full marks.

During the Ice Age glaciers scraped away the soil leaving areas of bare limestone exposed **(1)**. The limestone surface was then exposed to chemical weathering **(1)**. Cracks appear in the rock as it dries out **(1)**. Rainwater is a weak carbonic acid which reacts with the limestone as it passes through the rock **(1)**. It dissolves the stone, enlarging the joints and bedding planes **(1)**. The chemical weathering widens and deepens the cracks to form grykes **(1)**. This leaves exposed blocks of limestone called clints and the resulting pattern of blocks and spaces is called limestone pavement **(1)**.

4 marks

3 **Hint:** Make sure you read the question. This question is asking you to explain why features found on the map area are suitable for tourism. This means you must give reasons in your answer. Your answer must refer to map evidence. Giving an appropriate grid reference (preferably a six figure grid reference) will gain you a mark. The question refers to physical features found on the map. Do not talk about human features as this will not gain you any marks. Do not list the type of activities that you identify on the map – this is simple description. For example: 'The area can be used to ski, climb, sail, etc.' What you should say is: 'There are mountains in the area which have steep slopes which are good for skiing.' Name the feature on the map, then give the reason why it attracts tourists.

The steep slopes have been used for woodland which can be used for forest walks and orienteering **(1)**, for example the Glenmore Forest Park at 975109 **(1)**. There are many rivers in the area like the River Luineag which can be used for kayaking **(1)**. Lochs like Loch Morlich can be used for fishing and boating **(1)**. The steep mountain slopes can be used for rock climbing **(1)** and the corries and north facing slopes can be used for skiing at 990060 **(1)**. The beautiful scenery of the river valleys and the high mountains attract tourists. **(1)**

5 marks

4 **Hint:** Always read the question carefully. This question is asking about average UK temperatures so you need to talk about factors like latitude, altitude, etc. Do not talk about factors which affect temperature at one particular moment in time, for example the passage of a depression or an anticyclone.

Areas around London have a higher temperature than further north as it is closer to the Equator **(1)** so it gets more intense heating from the sun's rays as they are more concentrated **(1)**. Urban areas like London, Glasgow and Edinburgh have slightly higher average temperatures due to the heat island effect **(1)**. Places in northern Scotland are closer to the North Pole so have cooler average temperatures **(1)** as the sun's rays are less concentrated as they have more atmosphere to travel through **(1)**. The higher up you go the colder it gets so lower lying areas like Central Scotland are warmer than mountain areas like the north west Highlands **(1)** because temperatures drop by 1°C for every 100 metres in height **(1)**. Areas which are south facing are warmer because they get more sun **(1)** while north facing areas are colder because they experience cold northerly winds **(1)**. Western coastal areas are warmer because of a warm ocean current called the North Atlantic Drift **(1)**.

4 marks

5 **Hint:** In this type of question you need to explain the weather chart. You will not get full marks for simply describing the differences in the weather. Your answers must refer to the synoptic chart.

There is a cold front close to Belfast causing cloud cover and wind **(1)**. The isobars are closer together at Belfast so it will be experiencing stronger winds than Portsmouth **(1)**. The front is over Belfast so will be causing heavy rain **(1)**. Portsmouth is in the warm sector so it will be drier and clearer **(1)**. The isobars are further apart so it will be less windy **(1)**. The cold front has still not reached Portsmouth so the weather is more pleasant, allowing the race to go ahead **(1)**.

4 marks

Section 2: Human Environments

6   **Hint:** In this question you must use map evidence to answer the question. You need to give both advantages and disadvantages to gain full marks. You should put a six figure grid reference into your answer as this can gain you 1 mark.

Advantages:
There is flat/gently sloping land for building on **(1)**, built off the flood plain so little risk of flooding **(1)**. It is close to Aviemore so they will be able to access the amenities of the village, for example the railway station **(1)** at 895124 **(1)**. There is a road close by, the B970, giving access to Coylumbridge and Aviemore **(1)**.

Disadvantages:
Areas of forest would have to be cut down **(1)** destroying natural woodland and habitat for wildlife **(1)**. Increase in traffic on the only road bridge across the river would lead to congestion **(1)**. Electricity transmission line runs across the area so pylons would be an eyesore **(1)**.

5 marks

7   a)   **Hint:** In this question you must use figures and dates to gain full marks. Avoid describing one pyramid followed by the other. You need to make comparisons to get the marks. General statements like higher or lower/increasing or decreasing might only gain you 2 marks. Try to process the information in some way. Marks can be awarded for overall trends.

In 2010 there were about 152 million under the age of 10 but by 2050 it will be about 116 million **(1)**. In 2010 there were very few over 80 but by 2050 there will be about 114 million **(1)**. The number of young people will go down by 2050 **(1)**. In 2010 the highest age band was 20–24 but in 2050 it is 60–64 **(1)**. There are fewer males in 2050 in age group 0–4 dropping from 41 million to 30 million **(1)**.

3 marks

b)   **Hint:** Do not simply describe the changes to China's population. This will gain you little or no marks. You need to identify a change then explain the impact this change has on China.

More care will need to be provided for the elderly **(1)**, e.g. care homes **(1)**. There may not be enough carers for the elderly **(1)**. There will be a higher percentage of people in retirement with less working population to support them **(1)**. The government will struggle to find the extra money needed for the increased elderly population **(1)** leading to an increased strain on the already limited health services **(1)**. A reduction in the labour force will affect the economic growth rate **(1)**. Many buildings will be too big for the smaller number of school children **(1)**.

6 marks

8   **Hint:** Read the question – this question can also be asked for a developing country so be clear what area of the world you are writing about. You need to talk about two developments. If you only talk about one development you will lose marks – perhaps 2 marks.

If new technology chosen:
Machinery increases the efficiency on a farm enabling the farmer to plough, sow, spray, etc., more quickly, covering larger areas **(1)**. It also speeds up harvesting and results in the product being delivered to markets fresher **(1)** and at a higher premium **(1)**. It also allows for a smaller work force and therefore lower wage bills **(1)**. It allows for the use of satellite technology/computers to control the application of fertilisers to particular areas of fields, improving yields **(1)**.

If diversification chosen:
Farmers can obtain additional income from a variety of sources if they diversify their activities on the farm **(1)**. They may turn old farm workers' cottages into holiday chalets, may use part of the land for a golf course and may earn income from sports such as quad bike riding **(2)**. If crop yields are poor then farmers have another source of income to fall back on **(1)**.   **6 marks**

Section 3: Global Issues

9   **a)**   **Hint:** In this question you must use figures to gain full marks. General statements like higher or lower/increasing or decreasing might only gain you 2 marks. Do not describe China followed by United States. The question asks for differences so process the information you are given in some way to show this. For example, instead of saying China generates more renewable energy from hydroelectric sources (HEP) than the USA you could say China generates 86% of its renewable energy from HEP sources which is 25% more than the USA.

China generates 86% of its renewable energy from HEP which is 25% more than the USA **(1)**. China produces 1% of its renewable from solar tide and wave power whereas the USA produces none **(1)**. The USA produces 23% of its renewable energy from wind power compared to China at 9% **(1)**, a difference of 14% **(1)**. China produces none from geothermal power while the USA produces 3% **(1)**. China produces only 4% from biomass and waste which is 9% less than the USA **(1)**.   **4 marks**

b)   **Hint:** Avoid listing and describing. A simple list of methods will gain you only a few marks or none. This question asks for explanation so you need to give reasons. You should put as much detail into your answer as possible. Sometimes this question asks for physical causes or both human and physical so read the question. You will only get marks for the human causes and use valuable time which could be used to answer another question.

People generate large amounts of waste, including plastic, which remain in the environment for many years and release gases which contribute to greenhouse gases **(1)**. The production of electricity from fossil fuels like coal is responsible for the emission of huge amounts of greenhouse gases and other pollutants in the atmosphere **(1)**. Inappropriate disposal of items like fridges releases CFC gases into the atmosphere **(1)**. Increased use of timber for housing, etc., leads to the removal of huge numbers of trees which means that carbon is no longer absorbed by the trees **(1)** but instead trapped in the atmosphere, leading to global warming **(1)**. Population is growing in many parts of the world so more food is needed, leading to an increase in the amount of fertilisers used **(1)**, increasing the amount of nitrous oxide in the atmosphere **(1)**. Fumes from transport such as buses and cars release toxic gases into the atmosphere **(1)**.   **6 marks**

10 a) **Hint:** In this question you must use figures and months to gain full marks. General statements like higher or lower/increasing or decreasing might only gain you 2 marks. Try to process the information in some way. Marks can be awarded for overall trends. You must compare the graphs not simply describe one then the other.

Eismitte's highest temperature is 7 degrees centigrade more than Barrow's in July **(1)**. The lowest temperature in Barrow is -29 degrees in January compared to Eismitte at -27 degrees in February **(1)**, a difference of 2 degrees **(1)**. The range in temperature in Barrow is 34 degrees as opposed to 36 degrees in Eismitte **(1)**. Barrow has precipitation throughout the year, totalling 13 cm whereas there is less rainfall in Eismitte at around 9 cm **(1)**. Rainfall is lowest in the months of May, June and July in Eismitte where as it is highest in Point Barrows in June and August **(1)**. **4 marks**

b) **Hint:** To gain full marks for this question you need to mention both advantages and disadvantages. You should refer to specific case studies in your answer. Remember, the more detail in your answer the more marks you can achieve. A list of advantages and disadvantages will gain you only 1 or 2 marks. If you describe instead of explaining you may get no marks at all.

Advantages:
In Brazil large areas have been cleared by timber companies and the hardwood has been exported abroad increasing trade **(1)**. Brazil is a poor country and this is a way of earning money for the country **(1)**. Forests have been cleared to make room for new farmland to increase food production **(1)**. The land made available by removing the forest can be used for settlement for the expanding population **(1)**. Forests are also destroyed for mineral extractions which are also sold to other countries and provide employment for some local people **(1)**.

Disadvantages:
The habitats of wildlife are destroyed **(1)**. Burning trees release vast quantities of carbon dioxide into the atmosphere and may contribute to global warming **(1)**. The homes of indigenous tribes are destroyed **(1)** as is their traditional culture and way of life **(1)**. Plants which may contain cures for diseases are also destroyed **(1)**. Poor farmers lose their land and may be forced to migrate to towns and cities to find employment **(1)**. This increases the number of shanty towns **(1)**. **6 marks**

11 a) **Hint:** Remember, the map is there to help you answer the question. Try to name areas or countries in your answer. There are no marks for explanation, only for description, so do not explain your answer. Do not list places as this will gain you only 1 mark.

Hurricanes occur in the Caribbean in areas such as Jamaica **(1)**. They also occur along the south east coast of the USA affecting areas such as Florida and Mexico **(1)**. They move generally in a westerly direction **(1)**. Cyclones occur in an area stretching from Oceania to the south east coast of Africa **(1)**. Typhoons are found in South East Asia, stretching across the Indian Ocean to coastal India and Bangladesh **(1)**. **4 marks**

b) **Hint:** You should put as much detail into your answer as possible. You must refer to the effects on both people and the environment for full marks. You may lose a mark if you do not refer to examples you have studied in your answer.

Hurricane Dennis caused widespread flooding along the Gulf Coast of America and the Barrier Islands **(1)** forcing people to leave their homes and seek shelter further inland **(1)**. Homes and property were destroyed by the high winds and torrential rainfall, leaving people homeless **(1)**. Several people died and many were injured **(1)**. Farmland, power lines and bridges were destroyed **(1)**. Protected turtle nests on Marco Island beach were destroyed **(1)**. Roads were blocked with fallen trees causing disruption on the evacuation routes **(1)**. **6 marks**

12 a) Hint: In this question you must use figures to gain full marks. General statements like bigger than/smaller than might only gain you 2 marks. You should try to identify trends in your answer.

The EU exports a larger percentage of goods to the rest of the world than it imports **(1)**, the difference being 4.5% **(1)**. It exports 5% more than it imports from the USA **(1)**. It has a trade deficit with Russia **(1)**, exporting 6.9% but importing 12.3%, a difference of 5.4% **(1)**. It exports less to China than it imports by 8.1% **(1)**. There is a very small difference in its exports and imports to Japan with 0.3% more imports **(1)**. **4 marks**

b) Hint: The question asks for an explanation so make sure you don't just describe the benefits. Say what the benefit is, then say why it helps the people. Make sure you make enough points to gain 6 marks. Refer to specific examples you have studied as this adds detail to your answer.

Fair trade ensures the farmer a living wage **(1)**. More money goes directly to the farmer, as it cuts out the middlemen who skim off some of the profits **(1)**. Farmers receive a guaranteed minimum price so they are not affected as much by price fluctuations **(1)** and can receive some money in advance so they don't run short **(1)**. More of the money goes to the communities who can invest it in improving their living conditions **(1)**. Money can be used to provide electricity and drinking water or pay for education **(1)**. Fair trade also encourages farmers to treat their workers well and to look after the environment **(1)**. Often fair trade farmers are also organic farmers who do not use chemicals on their crops so protect the environment **(1)**. Health care services and education programmes are available and tackle the problems of HIV/AIDS **(1)**. **6 marks**

13 a) Hint: In this question you must use figures to gain full marks. General statements like higher or lower/increasing or decreasing might only gain you 2 marks. Try to process the information in some way. Marks can be awarded for overall trends. Remember, you need to compare as the question asks for differences.

The park with the highest number of visitors a year, visitor days a year and visitor spend a year is the Lake District **(1)**. The Lake District has 14 million more visitors a year than Dartmoor **(1)** and has nearly eight times as many visitor days **(1)**. It has more than ten times the income of Dartmoor **(1)**. The Cairngorms has only a third of the visitors a year that the Brecon Beacons gets **(1)** but earns just 12 million pounds less **(1)**. Dartmoor has more visitors per year than the Cairngorms but earns 74 million pounds less **(1)**. **4 marks**

b) Hint: Do not simply describe the growth of mass tourism – you need to explain why it happened. Use examples you studied in your answer. More detail equals more marks.

There is a wide range of ways to travel as a tourist and these methods are widely available **(1)**, for example car, boat and airplane **(1)**. Areas are better connected by roads and motorways so are more accessible **(1)**. The growth of budget airlines such as Easyjet and Ryanair have brought prices down and increased the number of people able to travel **(1)**. Holiday entitlement in many countries has increased over the past century which means that people can take more holidays during the year **(1)**. In many families both parents work so they have more money available to spend on holidays **(1)**. The average family size has decreased, making holidays more affordable to more people **(1)**. Package holidays are cheaper, so more accessible to more people, encouraging large numbers of people to travel **(1)**. Holiday programmes and advertising have encouraged people to travel **(1)**. **6 marks**

14 a) **Hint:** Remember, the map is there to help you answer the question. Try to name areas or countries in your answer as well as referring to percentages. There are no marks for explanation, only for description, so do not explain your answer. Do not list places as this will gain you only 1 mark.

Most of Africa south of the Sahara has over 80% risk of malaria **(1)** including Sahel countries like Sierra Leone and Chad **(1)**. Only two countries in Africa have under 20%, South Africa and Algeria **(1)**. Egypt, Libya and Tunisia are not endemic areas **(1)**. In South America only two countries have over 80% risk, Guyana and French Guiana **(1)**. Brazil, Peru and Venezuela have less than 20% risk **(1)**. The whole of India and Pakistan has over 80% risk **(1)**.   **4 marks**

b) **Hint:** Avoid listing. A simple list of effects will gain you only a few marks. You should put as much detail into your answer as possible. Try to refer to examples you have studied in your answer.

Malaria is the second biggest cause of death from infectious disease in African countries like Uganda and Nigeria **(1)**. 10 million days of school are missed each year in Africa because of malaria **(1)**. This leads to life-long learning disabilities **(1)**. Expectant mothers are vulnerable to malaria with risks to mothers and babies including low birth weight, miscarriage and maternal death **(1)**. Malaria can cost families up to 25% of their annual income **(1)** meaning parents might have to choose between treatment and food **(1)**. People cannot work so become even poorer **(1)**. Malaria decreases gross domestic product in countries with high disease rates. **(1)**   **6 marks**

C

Practice Paper C

Section 1: Physical Environments

1 a) **Hint:** First match the features you are sure are correct. You can then match any remaining feature to its reference. Do not leave a feature without a reference. Even if you do not know the correct answer take a guess at the remaining references as you could be lucky and match it correctly!

Headland: 570863

Stack: 612869

Bay: 535877   **3 marks**

   b) **Hint:** The more detail you put into an answer the more marks you will gain. If you simply refer to processes like erosion or deposition you will gain only 1 mark. However, you will gain additional marks if you explain the processes. You can gain a mark from drawing a series of diagrams which shows how the feature is formed at different stages. A diagram with labels which explain the formation can gain full marks.

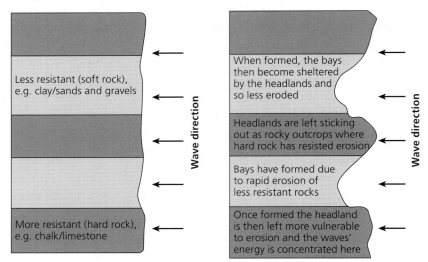

Headlands and bays are found in areas where there are bands of alternating hard and soft rock **(1)** which meet the coast at right angles **(1)**. The softer rock, for example clay, erodes more quickly, forming bays **(1)**, while the harder rock, for example chalk, erodes more slowly, forming headlands **(1)**. When formed the bays then become sheltered by the headlands as erode less **(1)**. Once formed the headland is then left more at risk from erosion as the waves' energy is concentrated here **(1)**.   **4 marks**

2 a) **Hint:** First match the features you are sure are correct. You can then match any remaining feature to its reference. Do not leave a feature without a reference. Even if you do not know the correct answer take a guess at the remaining references as you could be lucky and match it correctly!

V-shaped valley: 652516

Meander: 591515

Waterfall: 575535   **3 marks**

b) **Hint:** The more detail you put into an answer the more marks you will gain. You should mention processes in your answer. A list of processes like hydraulic action and corrosion will gain you just 1 mark. A detailed explanation of the processes will gain you more marks. You can gain a mark from drawing a series of diagrams which show how the feature is formed at different stages. A diagram with labels which explain the formation can gain full marks.

In the upper course, the water flows naturally downhill eroding the landscape vertically **(1)**. The river erodes a deep groove into the landscape using hydraulic action, corrasion and corrosion. As the river erodes downwards the sides of the valley are exposed to weathering which loosens the rocks and steepens the valley sides **(1)**. The rocks which fall into the river help with the process of corrasion which leads to further erosion **(1)**. The river transports the rocks downstream **(1)** and the channel becomes wider and deeper, creating a V-shaped valley between interlocking spurs **(1)**.   **4 marks**

3 **Hint:** This question is about how the physical landscape affects the land use. Make sure you don't simply describe the land use on the map. You need to identify a feature of the landscape from the map, then say what it's used for and why. For example: 'Feature of the landscape is flat land, identified land use – settlement – flat land good for building on.' You should also try to give a grid reference to identify the location you are discussing. Normally 1 mark is available for a grid reference, preferably a six figure grid reference at National 5.

The low lying flat land has encouraged the growth of settlements such as Swansea and Llanelli (5300) as it is suitable for building on **(1)**. Due to its coastal location it has allowed the development of docks at 672927 **(1)** enabling trade to take place **(1)**. Communication links, for example the vehicle ferry to Cork at 665924, have developed because of its coastal location **(1)**. Roads like the A406 have followed the natural routeway created by the River Afon Tawe **(1)**. The marshland found along the river estuary, for example at 5496, has prevented any building in that area **(1)**. The coastal area has encouraged the growth of tourism with many car parks, caravan/camp sites around Oxwich Bay (5186) **(1)**. The flat low lying land has encouraged arable farming to take place as the flat land allows machinery to be used **(1)**.   **5 marks**

4 **Hint:** Make sure you read the question carefully. In a weather question you should always look at the date of the chart as weather conditions will be different depending on the time of the year. You need to explain the problems/benefits brought by the high pressure not simply describe the weather. You need to mention both advantages and disadvantages for full marks.

Advantages:
The hot, dry weather allows people to enjoy outdoor activities like swimming and tennis, improving their health and wellbeing **(1)**. Sales of beach goods and ice cream may increase improving the profits of the local shops **(1)**. People can plan outdoor pursuits ahead as the air mass brings stable weather for some days **(1)**. The sunny weather encourages crops to ripen, increasing profit for farmers **(1)**.

Disadvantages:
This air mass can bring a prolonged spell of hot, dry weather which could cause drought **(1)** and can result in crops failing to thrive, reducing crop yield and income for farmers **(2)**, as well as decreasing the availability of some products in supermarkets **(1)**. Lack of rainfall can result in water levels falling in reservoirs causing hosepipe bans **(1)**. The dry summer weather encourages people to go outdoors and can result in people getting ill from dehydration and sunburn **(1)**. Thunderstorms may build up causing heavy downpours and damage from flash floods **(1)**.   **4 marks**

5 **Hint:** Read the question carefully. You must identify the landscape you are talking about in your answer or you may lose a mark. If you are asked for two land uses then you only need to write about how your two chosen land uses conflict and not all of them. This answer gives three examples of conflicts between different types of land users. You only chose two.

If upland limestone landscape chosen
If farming and industry chosen:
Areas of the Yorkshire Dales are used to quarry limestone and blasting to remove the rock can disturb farm animals **(1)** as well as cause sheep to miscarry their lambs **(1)**. Large, heavy lorries used to transport the limestone block the small country roads, hampering farmers from moving animals, equipment and products **(1)**. The blasting produces dust which can lie on the fields affecting crop growth **(1)**. The streams in the area can get polluted when the dust is washed into them making them unsuitable for animals to drink **(1)**.

Other examples could be:
If industry and recreation/tourism chosen:
Tourists/visitors may be restricted from visiting certain areas **(1)**. Noise from military operations may disturb visitors **(1)**. Military vehicles and tourist traffic may result in serious traffic congestion **(1)**

If recreation/tourism and farming chosen:
Walkers with dogs may worry sheep and cause them to miscarry **(1)** affecting the income of the farmer **(1)**. Tourists leave gates open allowing animals to escape **(1)** and drop litter which animals may eat **(1)**. Farmers may restrict access across their land **(1)**. **4 marks**

Section 2: Human Environments

6 **a)** **Hint:** Make sure you give actual map evidence. Do not use generic points in your answer.

The main transport links meet in this square **(1)**. There is a bus station **(1)** and there is a train station **(1)**. There are several churches **(1)** and a town hall **(1)**. **3 marks**

b) **Hint:** This question must be answered using map evidence. You need to give reasons for the location of these businesses on the edge of town. You need to give explanations, not just description. For example, instead of saying there is a road nearby (description) you should say there is a road nearby, the A725, which allows goods to be transported in and out. Since this is a map question you should try to use grid references, preferably a six figure reference, in your answer.

These developments like Kelvin Industrial Estate at 640525 are located on the edge of East Kilbride so land will be cheaper **(1)**. There is space available for expansion to the south of the industrial estate **(1)**. There are housing areas like Whitehills close by 635524 which can supply a labour force **(1)** as well as a market for its products **(1)**. The A726 runs close by allowing goods to be transported in and out of the area **(1)**. **5 marks**

7 **Hint:** You must use a specific example in your answer. You should put as much detail into your answer as possible.

If Kiberia, Nairobi chosen:

New roads are to be constructed to improve the transport of people and goods in the area **(1)**. Storm drains are to be built to control flooding **(1)**. Construction of piped water supply into the shanty **(1)** to reduce the chance of water borne diseases like cholera **(1)**. Construction of latrines to stop sewage contaminating the streets **(1)**. Slums will be cleared over a five year period **(1)** and people are being re-housed nearby in newly built apartments **(1)**. This is affordable accommodation and the estates also include schools, markets and other facilities **(1)**.

6 marks

8 **Hint:** This question asks for explanation so you need to give reasons in your answer. Description of stages 3 and 4 will get few if any marks. Make sure you refer to both stages in your answer.

In stage 3, the death rate continues to fall due to continued improvements in medicine **(1)** and increased standards of living **(1)**. The birth rate falls rapidly with the growth of family planning **(1)** and smaller families are needed as fewer babies die **(1)**. Population grows rapidly at the beginning of stage 3 due to the differences in the birth and death rates **(1)**, but growth levels off at the end of stage 3 as the birth rate and death rate reach similar low levels **(1)**.

In stage 4, a decreasing birth rate is shown with people wanting smaller (cheaper) families **(1)**, women following careers, greater access to family planning (contraception/abortion) **(2)**, a decreasing death rate and increasing life expectancy due to improved health care, sanitation, housing, food supply (2), pensions and care for the elderly **(1)**. Low birth rates and low death rates mean very low population growth **(1)**.

6 marks

Section 3: Global Issues

9 a) **Hint:** In this question you must use figures to gain full marks. General statements like higher or lower/increasing or decreasing might only gain you 2 marks. Do not describe one pie chart followed by the other. The question asks for differences so process the information you are given in some way. You could also mention trends in your answer.

The percentage of energy from fossil fuels will decrease from 78% in 2009 to 52% in 2020 **(1)**. Gas will decrease the most, falling from 45% to 29% **(1)** a difference of 16% **(1)**, whereas coal will fall by 10% **(1)**. Nuclear power has also decreased by 5% **(1)**. Renewable energy will increase from 6% to 31% **(1)** a difference of 25% **(1)**. **4 marks**

b) **Hint:** Remember not to describe or list the effects. You need to explain the effects. To gain full marks you need to mention the effects on both people and the environment as well as mentioning both local and global effects.

Increased temperatures are causing ice caps to melt so the habitats of animals like the polar bear are beginning to disappear **(1)**. Melting ice causes sea levels to rise **(1)** threatening coastal settlements like Bangladesh and the Netherlands **(1)**. Climate change could also affect weather patterns, leading to more droughts in areas of Africa **(1)** and more flooding in areas of the UK **(1)**. In the UK, some crops such as seed potatoes may not grow as well because of warmer and wetter conditions **(1)** but farmers may be able to grow different crops such as soft fruit in their place **(1)**. Some fish species may move further north affecting the livelihoods of fishermen in the UK **(1)**. **6 marks**

10 a) Hint: In this question you must use figures to gain full marks. General statements like higher or lower/increasing or decreasing might only gain you 2 marks.

Between 2001 and 2014 the overall trend is a decrease in tree loss **(1)**. The years with the greatest tree loss were 2004 and 2005 **(1)** with 2.5 million hectares lost in 2004 and 2.4 million lost in 2005 **(1)**. Tree loss decreased between 2005 and 2009 from 2.4 million hectares to 1 million hectares **(1)**, a decrease of 1.4 million hectares **(1)**. It then rose by 0.4 million in 2010 **(1)** before falling once again by just less than 0.4 million in 2011 **(1)**. It rose to 1.4 million in 2012 before falling once again to 1 million hectares in 2013 **(1)**. The trend is upwards again in 2014 increasing by 0.1 million **(1)**.   **4 marks**

b) Hint: The question asks for an explanation so make sure you don't just describe the land uses. Say what the land use is then say why it causes deforestation. Make sure you make enough points to gain 6 marks. Refer to specific examples you have studied as this adds detail to your answer.

Fires, mining, urbanisation, road construction and dams:
Large areas of the world's rainforest are destroyed every year by the deliberate burning of trees to create land for other uses, contributing to the greenhouse effect **(1)** as well as altering local climate **(1)**. Mining washes away the topsoil, destroying the growing environment of the trees **(1)**. Rivers are severely polluted causing further damage to the forest environment as well as making the water undrinkable for the indigenous people **(1)**. Trees are removed to create space for major highways, such as the Trans-Amazon Highway, but destroy the local habitat of plants and animals **(1)**. Huge areas of rainforest are flooded by building dams in order to create hydroelectric plants but flood large areas of rainforest, forcing the indigenous people to move away from their traditional hunting areas **(1)**. Settlements are built on the edge of the forest, destroying the natural habitat **(1)**.

Logging:
Trees are cut down both legally and illegally, reducing the biodiversity of the forest **(1)**. Animal habitats are destroyed and some animals could become extinct **(1)**. The logging operations destroy areas around the logged area, removing plants which could hold cures for diseases **(1)**.   **6 marks**

11 a) Hint: Remember, the map is there to help you answer the question. Try to name areas or countries in your answer. There are no marks for explanation, only for description, so do not explain your answer. Do not list places as this will gain you only 1 mark.

Earthquakes occur along or near the plate boundaries **(1)** in southern Europe, through the Middle East and into eastern and South East Asia **(1)**. There are also earthquakes stretching from Alaska down through the west coast of the USA, through Mexico and down the west coast of South America **(1)**. The main concentration of earthquakes is around the Pacific Ring of Fire **(1)**. There is a large concentration around the Indonesian islands **(1)**. There are some located in the north of India and the Himalayas **(1)**. In Africa most are located on the west coast and none on the east coast **(1)**.   **4 marks**

b) Hint: Do not list as this will gain you only 1 mark. The question asks for explanation so you must give reasons in your answer. State the method then say why it reduces the effects. Avoid describing. You need to refer to an example you have studied otherwise you may lose a mark. Examples given to tropical storms and earthquakes. You only need to answer on one disaster.

If earthquakes chosen answers may include:
In Japan earthquake drills are held so that people are aware of what to do in an earthquake **(1)**. Warning systems are put in place in order to give people some time to evacuate or move to a safer area **(1)** e.g. in Japan the government send warning texts

and broadcast warnings on TV **(1)**. Earthquake resistant buildings are built with deep foundations, shock absorbers and reinforced concrete **(1)** the buildings are designed to sway instead of collapsing so reducing the number of deaths and injuries **(1)**. Apartment buildings in Tokyo have sprinkler systems and gas cut-off valves to prevent fires spreading **(1)**. Earthquake survival kits containing bottled water, tinned food, torches are put together allowing people to survive till rescued **(1)**. Sea walls are built in coastal areas to protect the coastline from Tsunamis resulting from earthquakes at sea **(1)**.

For tropical storms answers may include:

In Hurricane Katrina satellite images provided advance warning allowing the population time to evacuate New Orleans **(1)** and protect buildings by boarding up windows and doors **(1)**. Public buildings were opened to allow people shelter from the storm **(1)**. People could prepare to protect themselves by building storm shelters under the ground **(1)**. Storm warnings were given over the radio or television **(1)**. Local people could stock up on food and water supplies for using until the storm had passed **(1)**. Local evacuation routes were well signposted ensuring people knew where to go if evacuation were needed **(1)**.   **6 marks**

12 a)   **Hint:** In this question you must use figures to gain full marks. General statements like higher or lower/increasing or decreasing might only gain you 2 marks.

The United States share of GDP changed from 29.7% in 2003 to 22.2% in 2013 **(1)** a drop of 7.5% in ten years **(1)**. The EU has the largest share of world trade in both 2003 and 2013 but this share has dropped 7% from 30.7% to 23.7% **(1)** China's share has nearly tripled from 4.3% to 12.1% **(1)** a rise of 7.8% **(1)**. The rest of the world's share has increased by 4.9% **(1)**. Canada and Mexico are no longer present in 2013 and are replaced by Russia and Brazil **(1)**.   **4 marks**

b)   **Hint:** This question asks for explanation so make sure you give reasons in your answer. Try to refer to an example/country you have studied. The more detail you give, the more marks you will achieve. Remember, for 6 marks you should make six points.

Ghana depends on cocoa for 85% of its exports and if the price of cocoa were to fall, cocoa farmers would receive less income **(1)**. They would have less to spend, affecting other businesses in Ghana **(1)**. They can find themselves with nothing to trade **(1)** and they are then forced to borrow money and end up in debt **(1)**. They then may have to borrow money to pay the debt, limiting their chances of development **(1)** and the chance to trade in higher priced manufactured goods **(1)**. If the price of the export in a developing country was to increase then there would be more income for the country to invest in other products and industries **(1)**. Countries would be less affected if they had a greater range of products to export **(1)** and this could lead to improvements in infrastructure, education and health.   **6 marks**

13 a)   **Hint:** In this question you must use figures to gain full marks. General statements like higher or lower/increasing or decreasing might only gain you 2 marks. Try to process the figures.

The number of tourist arrivals to Europe is expected to decrease from 50% to 41% **(1)**, a drop of 9% **(1)**. The greatest increase in tourist arrivals is in Asia and the Pacific from 22% to 29% **(1)**, a rise of 7% **(1)**. The Americas have decreased by 3% **(1)**. Both the Middle East and Africa have increased **(1)** with Africa slightly more and now equalling the Middle East **(1)**.   **4 marks**

b)   **Hint:** Try to relate the question to an area you have studied. You may lose a mark if you do not refer to a named example. Mention examples in your answer. You should make reference to both the people and the environment.

Ecotourism, in countries such as South Africa, helps the people of a developing country by bringing more money into the economy **(1)**. It provides financial benefits to local people **(1)**, e.g. jobs as tour guides **(1)**, and gives them some control over developments in their home area **(1)**. Ecotourism aims to minimise the impact of tourism on an area **(1)**. It promotes responsible travel to natural areas and conserves the environment **(1)**. It raises awareness of the natural environment and the culture of the area **(1)**. Some of the money raised from this type of tourism is used for conservation of the area and its people's way of life **(1)**. Ecotourism tries to ensure that the tourists have a positive experience without negatively affecting the local people and the environment **(1)**. Money from tourism helps to improve the local and natural environment by ensuring beaches remain clean, historic buildings and sites are maintained and wildlife and safari parks are set up to protect the local wildlife **(1)**.   **6 marks**

14 a) **Hint:** This is a difficult question to answer. At National 5 you are expected to know the names of the continents and some countries. This question lends itself to giving a list of countries. As long as you relate your list to the level of obesity as shown in the answer this will be acceptable.

The main areas of obesity in the world with over 25% include USA, Canada, Australia and New Zealand **(1)**. In Europe the main obese areas with over 25% are the UK, the Czech Republic and the island of Mallorca **(1)**. In South America there are no countries with over 25% **(1)** with most countries including Brazil having between 15% and 24.9% **(1)**. Bolivia, Paraguay, Ecuador and Guyana have less obesity with 5% to 14.9% **(1)**. In Africa, only Libya has more than 25% obesity **(1)**. Many countries, including the Sahel zone as well as central and eastern Africa, have less than 5% obesity **(1)**. The whole of India, Bangladesh and Pakistan are less than 5% **(1)**.   **4 marks**

b) **Hint:** This question lends itself to a list. Try to avoid this. Try to expand your answer to explain the effect on the heart – for example 'over eating' can be expanded into 'over eating causes obesity and the extra weight carried puts a strain on the heart'.

If heart disease chosen:
Heart disease can be inherited from parents so predisposes a person to developing the disease **(1)**. Over-eating can lead to obesity, putting extra pressure on the heart **(1)**. Smoking narrows the arteries and affects the lungs **(1)**. This can lead to a condition known as emphysema, putting a strain on the heart by making it work faster **(1)**. The build-up of fatty deposits on the walls of the arteries restricts the flow of blood to the heart **(1)**. Lack of exercise raises blood pressure, affecting the efficiency of the heart **(1)**. Poor diet increases cholesterol which furs up and narrows the arteries **(1)**. Stress leads to high blood pressure resulting in the heart having to work faster **(1)**.   **6 marks**